2001 SUPPLEMENT
CASES AND MATERIALS ON
AMERICAN PROPERTY LAW
Third Edition

By

Sheldon F. Kurtz
Percy Bordwell Professor of Law
University of Iowa Law School

Herbert Hovenkamp
Ben V. & Dorothy Willie Professor of Law
University of Iowa Law School

AMERICAN CASEBOOK SERIES®

WEST GROUP
A THOMSON COMPANY

ST. PAUL, MINN., 2001

West Group has created this publication to provide you with accurate and authoritative information concerning the subject matter covered. However, this publication was not necessarily prepared by persons licensed to practice law in a particular jurisdiction. West Group is not engaged in rendering legal or other professional advice, and this publication is not a substitute for the advice of an attorney. If you require legal or other expert advice, you should seek the services of a competent attorney or other professional.

American Casebook Series, and the West Group symbol
are registered trademarks used herein under license.

COPYRIGHT © 2001 By WEST GROUP
                        610 Opperman Drive
                        P.O. Box 64526
                        St. Paul, MN 55164–0526
                        1–800–328–9352

All rights reserved
Printed in the United States of America

ISBN 0–314–26021–8

TEXT IS PRINTED ON 10% POST
CONSUMER RECYCLED PAPER

TABLE OF CONTENTS

(Including New and Retitled Sections)

	Page
Chapter 1. Acquisition of Property Rights: A First Look	1

Sec.
1.3	Acquisition of Property Rights by Capture	1
1.4	Acquisition of Property Rights by Find	1
1.6	Acquisition of Property Rights by Creation	2
1.7	Acquisition of Property Rights by Gift	2
	In Re Estate of Smith	2
	Notes and Questions	7

Chapter 3. Adverse Possession — 8

Sec.
3.2	The Actual, Open, Continuous and Exclusive Requirements	8
3.3	State of Mind	9
3.4	Adverse Possession of Chattels	10

Chapter 4. Estates in Land and Future Interests — 11

Sec.
4.3	Fee Simple Determinable and Fee Simple on Condition Subsequent	11
	Pricokorn v. Maloof	11
4.8	The Rule in Shelley's Case	17
	In The Matter of the Estate of Hendrickson	17
4.10	The Rule Against Perpetuities	21

Chapter 7. Leasehold Estates — 22

Sec.
7.9	Retaliatory Eviction	22
7.11	Termination of Leasehold Estates and Reversion Of the Premises	23
	Stonehedge Square Limited Partnership v. Movie Merchants, Inc.	23
	Aurora Business Park Associates v. Michael Albert, Inc.	27

Chapter 8. "Private" Controls of Land Use: Servitudes — 33

Sec.
8.2	The Creation of Servitudes	33
	8.2.4. Prescription	33
	8.2.5. Recognition of Public Access Rights: Implied Dedication, Custom, and the "Public Trust"	34
8.4	Transfer of Obligations and Benefits	35
	8.4.2. Real Covenants and Equitable Servitudes: Traditional Doctrine and Modern Deviations	35

TABLE OF CONTENTS

Sec.

		Page
8.4.3	Implied Burdens	36

Chapter 10. Takings, Deliberate and Inadvertent — 37

Sec.

10.1	Eminent Domain		37
	10.1.1	"Public Use"	37
10.2	Inverse Condemnation		38
	10.2.2	Taking by Regulation	38
		City Of Monterey v. Del Monte Dunes at Monterey, Ltd.	38
		Notes and Questions	44
	10.2.3	Remedies for Unconstitutional Takings	48

Chapter 11. "Public" Controls of Land Use: An Introduction to Zoning and Land Use Planning — 49

Sec.

11.2	Legitimate Rationales of Zoning Law		49
	11.2.1	Federal Law: Zoning Limiting Expression, or Regulating Indecency and Excess?	49
		City of Erie v. Pap's A.M. DBA "Kandyland"	49
		Notes and Questions	55
	11.2.2.	The Role of State Law: Regulating Relationships and Aesthetics	56
11.4	Settled Expectations and the Zoning Process		57
	11.4.3.	Nonconforming Uses	57

Chapter 12. The Law of Housing Discrimination — 58

Sec.

12.3.	Housing Discrimination and Federal Law: The 1866 Civil Rights Act and the 1968 Fair Housing Act	58
12.4	Housing Discrimination and State Law	59

2001 SUPPLEMENT TO CASES AND MATERIALS ON
AMERICAN PROPERTY LAW

Third Edition

*

Chapter 1

ACQUISITION OF PROPERTY RIGHTS: A FIRST LOOK

§ 1.3 ACQUISITION OF PROPERTY RIGHTS BY CAPTURE

Add at end of note 15 on page 19:

In Lamare v. North Country Animal League, 170 Vt. 115, 743 A.2d 598 (1999) plaintiff's dog escaped and ultimately was turned over to the local pound which put the dog up for adoption in accordance with the authority granted to it by a local ordinance. The pound refused not only to recognize plaintiff's ownership claim based upon AKC papers but also denied plaintiff's application to "adopt" the dog on the grounds that the dog's best interest would not be served by allowing the plaintiff to adopt the dog. Plaintiff's suit to recover the dog failed on the grounds that the defendant's action, while insensitive, nonetheless complied with the local ordinance. The court suggested that plaintiff might have an action to recover damages for emotional distress.

§ 1.4 ACQUISITION OF PROPERTY RIGHTS BY FIND

Add as Note (h) immediately following (g) on page 54:

(h) A was employed by Y to renovate the rooms in Y's hotel. While renovating one room A removed ceiling tiles and found a box near a heating duck with $50,000. A claims title to the money as a "finder." Is the property lost or abandoned (finder wins) or mislaid (Y wins). See Terry v. A.D. Lock, Lock Hospitality, Inc., 343 Ark. 452, 37 S.W.3d 202 (2001).

§ 1.6 ACQUISITION OF PROPERTY RIGHTS BY CREATION

Add as new note 6A immediately following note 6 on page 118:

Both the Kass and Davis courts supported the proposition that the parties to the IVF agreement could agree to a disposition of the embryos in the event of their divorce. However, in A.Z. v. B.Z, 431 Mass. 150, 160, 725 N.E.2d 1051, 1057 (2000) the Massachusetts high court stated that "even had the husband and the wife entered into an unambiguous agreement ... regarding the disposition of the frozen preembryos, we would not enforce an agreement that would compel one donor to become a parent against his or her will.... [F]orced procreation is not an area amenable to judicial enforcement. It is well established that courts will not enforce contracts that violate public policy."

In Litowitz v. Litowitz, 102 Wash. App. 934, 10 P.3d 1086 (App. 2000), appeal pending, husband and wife entered into an agreement regarding cryopreservation of preembryos produced with the husband's sperm and eggs from an egg donor (not the wife). Since the wife was not a gamete provider, the court held that her interest in procreation was non-existent and that the husband as the only progenitor before the court had sole control over the disposition of the embryos.

§ 1.7 ACQUISITION OF PROPERTY RIGHTS BY GIFT

Add as a new case following Foster v. Reiss on page 140

IN RE ESTATE OF SMITH

Superior Court of Pennsylvania (1997).
694 A.2d 1099.

DEL SOLE, JUDGE:

On May 7, 1994, Appellant's husband, Alfred E. Smith (Decedent), committed suicide in the basement of the couple's home. Prior to his suicide, Decedent took the following steps in an effort to attend to several of his personal affairs. On May 5, 1994, Decedent drafted four checks in various amounts to four individuals: Joy Youpa (Decedent's girlfriend), Carol Sandt (Ms. Youpa's sister), Barbara Kressley (Decedent's sister), and Diana Kressley (Decedent's niece). On May 6, 1994 Decedent prepared and executed a holographic will. The will contained the following contested provision: "I want Willard Kressley to have the option of buying my '66 Corvette from Jean [Appellant] for $12,000." Also on May 6, 1994, Decedent mailed the checks to his sister and niece accompanied with a suicide note.[1] On May 7, 1994, before committing suicide, Decedent delivered the checks to his girlfriend and her sister by

---

1. The note stated:

I know this is a hell of a mess and I am truly sorry for the embarrassment, but I

leaving the checks under a pizza box on their kitchen table. The two mailed checks and the note were received on May 9, 1994, two days after the suicide. Each of the recipients knew of Decedent's death at the time she cashed her check.

After Appellant, as administratrix of Decedent's estate, discovered that Decedent had written the four checks, she requested that the funds be returned by the recipients to the estate. The four recipients refused and Appellant commenced a civil action alleging conversion and seeking restitution ...

The court entered a decree holding that the four checks to the donees were valid gifts causa mortis and that Mr. Kressley was not entitled to the Corvette. Appellant and Cross–Appellant filed exceptions to the decree nisi which were denied. These appeals followed ...

To establish a gift causa mortis, it must be shown that at the time of the alleged gift, the decedent intended to make a gift, the decedent apprehended death, the res of the intended gift was either actually or constructively delivered, and death actually occurred. *In re Ream's Estate,* 413 Pa. 489, 490, 198 A.2d 556, 557 (1964) It is not necessary that the donor expressly say he knows or believes he is dying, that may be inferred from the attendant circumstances. It will suffice if at the time the gift was made, the donor believed he was going to die, that he was likely to die soon; and death did actually ensue within a reasonable time thereafter. *Titusville Trust Co. v. Johnson,* 375 Pa. 493, 499, 100 A.2d 93, 97 (1953).

The facts of the instant case support a finding of a gift causa mortis. On May 5, 1994, Decedent wrote and executed the four checks to four separate individuals in various specific amounts. On May 6, 1994, Decedent mailed two of the checks, accompanied by a note of suicide. On May 7, 1994, Decedent physically delivered the other two checks, and then, sadly, took his own life. All of the requisite elements of a gift causa mortis have been established. Therefore, the lower court was correct in refusing to revoke the checks.[2]

CIRILLO, PRESIDENT JUDGE EMERITUS, concurring and dissenting.

I agree that Mr. Kressley is entitled to receive the 1966 Corvette as a direct gift under the decedent's will. I vehemently disagree, however, with the majority's incomplete analysis and inaccurate conclusion that

can't go on. I know there will be legal questions about the will, but they are my intentions. I know the estate taxes for the state could have been avoided, but I don't have time. *I'm sorry. I'm sorry. I'm sorry.*
Good-bye
Alfred

Barbara,
The checks are [to] use at your discretion.
Alfred

2. We believe that by considering gifts made in contemplation of suicide to be gifts causa mortis, we further the public policy against suicide since the donor may retrieve the gifts if the suicide is not completed. As our courts have held, a gift causa mortis differs from other gifts only in that it is made when the donor believes he is about to die, and is revocable should he survive. *Titusville Trust Co. v. Johnson,* at 497–498, 100 A.2d at 96. *See, In re Brown's Estate,* 489 Pa. 199, 413 A.2d 1083 (1980).

the decedent made valid *gifts causa mortis* of the four checks. For this reason, I would reverse that portion of the trial court's decree affirming the gift of the checks to the intended donees.

A recitation of the details behind the death of the decedent is needed for a complete understanding of the lack of the proper donative intent for valid *gifts causa mortis*. On May 7, 1994, appellant's husband, Mr. Alfred E. Smith, committed suicide in the basement of the their Allentown home. Decedent's expired body was found lying on a 3 x 6 foot piece of carpet, his head resting on a throw pillow.

Prior to his death, decedent wrote four checks to four different individuals in varying amounts. He left two of the checks on a kitchen table, under a pizza box, in the home of one of the donees. The remaining checks were mailed to the donees by the decedent. All four checks were dated May 5, 1994; two of the donees received their checks on May 7th, the remaining on May 10th. On May 9th, two donees cashed their checks, another donee cashed hers on May 10th and the last cashed her check on May 11th. Each recipient, at the time she cashed her check, knew that Mr. Smith had passed away.

After Appellant discovered that decedent had issued the four checks, she, as administratrix of decedent's estate, requested that the recipients return the check proceeds to the estate. When the four donees refused, Appellant instituted a civil action alleging conversion and seeking restitution.

On December 12, 1995, Judge Robert Young entered a decree determining, among other things, that the four contested checks were valid *gifts causa mortis*. Appellant and cross-appellant filed exceptions to the *decree nisi, see* Pa.R.C.P. 227.1, which were denied . . .

The question of whether the evidence of a gift satisfies the legal standard is always a question of law for the court's determination. *Titusville Trust Co. v. Johnson,* 375 Pa. 493, 100 A.2d 93 (1953). To constitute a complete "gift," there must be a purpose to give, expressed in words or signs and executed by the actual delivery of the thing given to a donee or someone for the donee's use. *Id.* at 496–98, 100 A.2d at 96. A *gift causa mortis* is defined as:

> A gift made when the donor believes he is about to die, . . . and a gift made by a person in his last illness, or in danger of death, subject to the implied condition that if the donor shall recover, of if the donee die[s] first, the gift shall be void, . . . and a gift made in contemplation of death with the right to revoke if the donor should survive.

17 P.L.E. § 11. A claimant of a *gift causa mortis* has the burden of proving the requisite elements of such a gift by clear, direct, precise, and convincing evidence. *In re Ream's Estate,* 413 Pa. 489, 198 A.2d 556 (1964). A *gift causa mortis* differs from other gifts, namely *inter vivos* gifts, only in that it is made when the donor believes he is about to die and is revocable if he survives. *Titusville,* 375 Pa. at 493, 100 A.2d at 93.

Accordingly, the element of delivery requires the same proof for an *inter vivos* gift or a *gift causa mortis. McHale v. Toole,* 258 Pa. 293, 101 A. 988 (1917).

The testimony reveals the following uncontroverted facts: all four checks were written by decedent before his death; all four checks, before decedent's death, were either put into the U.S. mail or left in a donee's home, by decedent, for the donees; there was no consideration given for the checks; all donees knew of the decedent's death at the time they cashed the checks; and, the checks were not cashed until after the decedent's death.

In *In Fleigle Estate,* 13 Fid.2d 141, *affirmed on other grounds,* 444 Pa.Super. 632, 664 A.2d 612 (1995) (*en banc*), the court of common pleas was faced with a situation factually similar to the present case. In *Fleigle,* the decedent had committed suicide and left a gift of two checks, to donees, on the counter in his own apartment. The court found that the checks, which were not negotiated by the donees until *after* the death of the decedent, were sufficiently delivered and that a valid *gift causa mortis* existed. Accordingly, the Fleigle estate was not entitled to recover the funds represented by the checks.

The court of common pleas' decision in *Fleigle's Estate,* while not binding authority on this court, is the only Pennsylvania case addressing the situation of a *gift causa mortis* where the donor has died by committing suicide. Although the appellant and the trial court fail to discuss whether a decedent who commits suicide can have the requisite intent necessary to feel that he or she is making a gift "in contemplation of death," I find that an answer to this question is central to a determination of whether a *gift causa mortis* was made in the present case. It is the majority's cursory reference to this issue that compels me to dissent and express my views on the far-reaching and negative effects that this case will have on the law of this Commonwealth.

It is well established that a *gift causa mortis* is premised upon the fact that the donor/decedent *must* be making the gift while in his last illness or in "periculo mortis."[3] *Michener v. Dale,* 23 Pa. 59 (1854). Our supreme court has held that a conditional gift made by a soldier going off to war is not a valid *gift causa mortis;* such a donor is not "under apprehension of death." *Linsenbigler v. Gourley,* 56 Pa. 166 (1867). A gift while a donor is in full health has also been declared void for purposes of establishing a gift of bonds as a *donatio causa mortis. Stockham's Estate,* 6 Dist. 196 (1897). It should be noted, however, that in order for a donor to be "in apprehension of death," one's illness need not be so extreme as in the case of proving an oral will made by a testator in his last sickness, before witnesses, and then later reduced to writing. *See Stackhouse's Estate,* 23 D. & C. 322 (1935) (even though decedent was optimistic concerning her recovery from illness at the time she gave a car as a gift to a donee, decedent did "act in apprehension of death" and gift was valid *donatio causa mortis* when donor died two

---

3. This term is Latin for "in danger of death."

days later); *see also Lawrence v. Hartford Nat. Bank and Trust Co.*, 24 Conn.Supp. 419, 193 A.2d 506 (1963) (gift need not be made while decedent confined to bed; valid *gift causa mortis* made when 72 year-old woman, suffering a serious hip fracture, died after having surgery; surgery was made necessary by a present disease).

Because the intention to commit suicide may be readily abandoned at one's own will, courts from other jurisdictions have taken the position that the contemplated or intended suicide of a donor is not a "peril, ailment or disease" which can serve as the foundation of a *gift causa mortis*. 60 A.L.R.2d § 2 at 577; *see also Ray v. Leader Federal Savings & Loan Assoc.*, 40 Tenn.App. 625, 645, 292 S.W.2d 458, 467 (1953) ("[s]ickness, peril and danger, as used in definitions of donations *causa mortis* we believe to mean something other than a determination of an individual who is presumed to be well, physically and mentally, to take his life.").[4] See also 38 Am.Jur. 2D *Gifts* § 10 (1968); Black's Law Dictionary 1286 (5th ed. 1979) (suicide is "[s]elf-destruction; the deliberate termination of one's existence."). Courts, therefore, have found that gifts made in contemplation of suicide are against public policy and should not be enforced. *See, e.g., Ray, supra.*

The Pennsylvania Supreme Court has held that the law does not look with favor upon *gifts causa mortis;* these gifts are often made without the regular safeguards afforded by the law for the disposition of property in an executed will. *Hawn v. Stoler,* 208 Pa. 610, 57 A. 1115 (1904). In keeping with this view, strict proof is required to find that such gifts exist.

Without any instructive guide from case law of this jurisdiction on the issue of gifting in contemplation of suicide, I am forced to broaden my search and delve into Pennsylvania's general public policy with regard to condoning the commission of suicide. My research locates a case which briefly discusses this jurisdiction's view on suicide. In *Commonwealth v. Root,* 191 Pa.Super. 238, 156 A.2d 895 (1959), the court, in dicta, outlined the civil ramifications of suicide and the general policy concerns behind taking life at one's own hands. The *Root* court stated:

> If a man's negligence contributes to his injury or death, he, or those claiming under him, cannot recover damages in a civil suit. It has long been the policy of the common law that one who fails to look out for his own safety is not entitled to demand in court that he be

---

4. I recognize that there are jurisdictions that would find that contemplation of suicide is sufficient for purposes of proving an element of a *gift causa mortis*. See *Scherer v. Hyland,* 75 N.J. 127, 380 A.2d 698 (1977); *see also Berl v. Rosenberg,* 169 Cal.App.2d 125, 336 P.2d 975 (1959) (public policy against suicide will not invalidate and otherwise valid *gift causa mortis*); *In re Van Wormer's Estate,* 255 Mich. 399, 238 N.W. 210 (1931) (melancholia ending in suicide sufficient to sustain a *gift causa mortis*). These courts have focused on the fact that according to modern human psychological principles, the utter despair attendant upon one contemplating suicide may reasonably be viewed as even more imminent than a person struggling with a fatal physical illness. Such reasoning is attenuated, at best, in light of this Commonwealth's consistent views disfavoring suicide.

compensated for the consequences of his failure.... The policy of the law is to protect human life, even the life of a person who wishes to destroy his own.

Id. at 244, 156 A.2d at 899–900.

Pennsylvania's policy of protecting human life is further evidenced by the criminalization of assisted suicide in our Criminal Code. *See* 18 Pa.C.S.A. § 2505 (causing or aiding suicide). Unlike the majority, I find that it would be prudent to adopt the reasoning of other jurisdictions that render alleged *gifts causa mortis* void when they are made in contemplation of suicide. I find further support for adopting this view in light of the strict proof requirement promulgated by our highest state court in order to establish a valid *gift causa mortis,* as well as the disfavored disposition of property outside of a will. Such suicide gifts are not intended to be in apprehension of an impending illness; rather, they are completely voluntary, controlled by the will of the donor, and easily subject to change by the decision to not take one's own life.

In line with my conclusion, I cannot agree with the majority's convoluted reasoning, contained in a mere footnote, which states that:

> We believe that by considering gifts made in contemplation of suicide to be *gifts causa mortis,* we further the public policy against suicide since the donor may retrieve the gifts if the suicide is not completed.

By upholding and validating gifts made in contemplation of suicide, the majority rewards the donor and his or her donees for the intended and successful completion of a self-destructive act. Furthermore, in response to the majority's above-quoted language, I find that it is just as reasonable to conclude that a donor's intent to commit suicide while in the process of disposing of his or her property is as strong as, if not stronger than, his or her intent to retrieve and repossess the gifts upon a change in one's will to commit the act. The majority's holding cuts against the notion that courts prefer the reliable disposition of property through a will or by the well-expressed intentions in a living person's *inter vivos* transfer.

I, therefore, respectfully dissent.

Notes and Questions

Suppose O, who is dying from cancer, on his deathbed gives A a check for $5,000. A fails to cash the check before O dies two days later. Following O's death, the bank on which the check is drawn honors the check. The administrator of O's estate then sues A to recover the $5,000. What result? See Woo v. Smart, 247 Va. 365, 442 S.E.2d 690 (Va. 1994).

Chapter 3

ADVERSE POSSESSION

§ 3.2 THE ACTUAL, OPEN, CONTINUOUS AND EXCLUSIVE REQUIREMENTS

Add as note 16 on page 192:

Who should bear the burden of proof in adverse possession cases? Most, if not all courts, agree that the adverse possessor bears the burden. To meet that burden, is it sufficient that the possessor satisfy the elements by a preponderance of the evidence. Consider the following passage from Brown v. Gobble, 196 W.Va. 559, 474 S.E.2d 489, 493–94 (1996):

> The first argument raised by the defendants is that the circuit court committed error by requiring them to prove adverse possession by clear and convincing evidence . . .
>
> There is a minority view that a preponderance of the evidence is sufficient to establish adverse possession . . . There is little reason given for adopting this standard other than it is the usual rule in civil cases.
>
> On the other hand, the view adopted by a majority of jurisdictions is that adverse possession must be shown by clear and convincing evidence . . . Carpenter v. Ruperto, 315 N.W.2d 782 (Iowa 1982).
>
> It is appropriate, in our opinion, that adverse possession be proved by a more stringent standard than a mere preponderance of the evidence. . . .
>
> [O]n policy grounds there is sound and reasonable justification for the majority view. The function of a standard of proof is to "instruct the factfinder concerning the degree of confidence our society thinks he [or she] should have in the correctness of a factual conclusion for a particular kind of adjudication." In re Winship, 397 U.S. 358, 370, 90 S.Ct. 1068, 1076, 25 L.Ed.2d 368 (1970) (Harlan, J. Concurring). "The standard [of proof] serves to allocate the risk of error between the litigants and to indicate the relative importance attached to the ultimate decision." Addington v. Texas, 441 U.S. 418, 423 . . . (1979).
>
> While the preponderance standard applies across the board in civil cases, a higher standard is needed where fairness and equity require

more persuasive proof.... Although the standard clear and convincing is less commonly used, it nonetheless is no stranger to West Virginia civil cases. In Wheeling Dollar Sav. & Trust Co. v. Singer, 162 W.Va. 502, 510, 250 S.E.2d 369, 374 (1978), this Court stated that "clear and convincing" is the measure or degree of proof that will produce in the mind of the factfinder a firm belief or conviction as to the allegations sought to be established. It should be the highest possible standard of civil proof. Cramer v. Dep't of Hwys., 180 W.Va. 97, 99 n. 1, 375 S.E.2d 568, 570 n. 1 (1988). The interest at stake in an adverse possession claim is not the mere loss of money as is the case in the normal civil proceedings. Rather, it often involves the loss of a homestead, a family farm or other property associated with traditional family and societal values. To this extent, most courts have used the clear and convincing standard to protect these important property interests ... Adopting the clear and convincing standard of proof is more than a mere academic exercise. At a minimum, it reflects the value society places on the rights and interests being asserted.

The bottom line is that the function of the legal process is to minimize the risk of erroneous decisions ... The law should not allow the land of one to be taken by another, without a conveyance or consideration, merely upon slight presumption or probabilities. The relevant evidence in an adverse action must necessarily expand over a ten year period. A preponderance standard, in our judgment, would create the risk of increasing the number of cases whereby land is erroneously taken from the title owner under spurious adverse possession claims. This heightened standard of clear and convincing is one way to impress the factfinder with the importance of the decision, and thereby reduce the chances that spurious claims of adverse possession will be successful. Having concluded that the preponderance standard falls short of meeting the demands of fairness and accuracy in the factfinding process in the adjudication of adverse possession claims, we hold that the burden is upon the party who claims title by adverse possession to prove by clear and convincing evidence all elements essential to such title. To the extent that a different standard is intimated in our previous decisions, we herein expressly reject such intimations.

§ 3.3 STATE OF MIND

Add as Note 6 on page 204:

6. Should there be a presumption that a possession that is actual, open, notorious, exclusive and continuous is not hostile where the true owner and the possessor are closely related to each other? See, Totman v. Malloy, 431 Mass. 143, 725 N.E.2d 1045 (2000) (court refuses to find a presumption that possession by a close family member is presumptively permissive).

§ 3.4 ADVERSE POSSESSION OF CHATTELS

Add to Note 3 on Page 221:

In Songbyrd, Inc. v. Estate of Albert B. Grossman, 23 F.Supp. 2d 219 (N.D.N.Y.1998) the court held that the statute of limitations for conversion ran from the time of the conversion, at least when sued was brought against the converter or its successor in interest. The court noted that the Guggenheim case which adopted the "demand and refusal" rule applied as against a defendant who was a bona fide purchaser, not when the defendant was the thief.

Chapter 4

ESTATES IN LAND AND FUTURE INTERESTS

§ 4.3 FEE SIMPLE DETERMINABLE AND FEE SIMPLE ON CONDITION SUBSEQUENT

PRIESKORN v. MALOOF

Court of Appeals of New Mexico (1999).
128 N.M. 226, 991 P.2d 511.

BUSTAMANTE, J.

Plaintiff Mia Prieskorn (Prieskorn) appeals from a judgment refusing to quiet title to certain property in San Miguel County, New Mexico. She contends on appeal that (1) a reversionary clause in a deed affecting a portion of her property unreasonably restrains alienation of her property, and (2) changes in the circumstances of the subject property and its environs are so profound and substantial that enforcement of the reversionary clause would be inequitable. We affirm.

BACKGROUND

Prieskorn was the owner of two parcels of land situated in San Miguel County, consisting of a total of approximately 26.46 acres. A portion of Prieskorn's land is located within a larger surveyed tract of land consisting of seventy-one acres as described and included in a warranty deed from Najeeb and Mentaha Maloof to the City of Las Vegas (Najeeb Deed), dated December 24, 1935, and recorded January 17, 1936, in the office of the San Miguel County clerk. The Najeeb Deed contains the following restriction:

> provided, however, that this conveyance is hereby made and the land conveyed under the following conditions: That no building now on said premises or to be erected on said land shall at any time be used for immoral purposes, or for the manufacture and/or sale of any intoxicating liquors by the grantee, its successors, heirs, and assigns, and that in the event of said condition being broken, then this deed

shall become null, void, and of no effect, and all right, title, and interest of, in and to the premises of said above described land hereby conveyed, shall revert to the grantor, his successors and assigns.

The reversionary clause establishes Defendants' interest in the land because, should the reversionary condition be broken, title to the property might revert to Najeeb and Mentaha Maloof, their successors and assigns . . .

Since 1961, the land conveyed in the Najeeb Deed has been subdivided into multiple ownership with a housing development of thirty homes on the west end and a 204–unit mobile home park constructed by Prieskorn's parents and predecessors-in-interest on the east end. The center portion is undeveloped. To date, there have apparently been no violations of the provisions of the reversionary clause and thus no efforts to enforce it. Nevertheless, Prieskorn argues that she has been unable to obtain title insurance on the property because of the existence of the reversionary clause. She argues in turn that this has adversely affected the value of her property. She provided no evidence that the values of other properties encompassed by the Najeeb Deed have been adversely affected by the reversionary clause.

DISCUSSION

Before turning to the issues we think it important to define the property interests created by the Najeeb Deed. Clearly, by the insertion of the restriction in the deed the grantors meant to convey something less than a fee simple estate—either a fee simple determinable with an associated possibility of reverter or a fee simple on condition subsequent and right of entry, which is also sometimes referred to as a right of reentry or power of termination.

> No exact language is required to create a determinable fee or a condition subsequent, but there must be a clear indication in the dedication of an intent that an interest is given or granted as a determinable fee or on condition subsequent. . . . "[A] possibility of reverter is that future interest which a transferor keeps when he transfers an estate and attaches a special limitation which operates in his own favor." When this type of interest is created, the grantee's estate automatically terminates upon the happening of an event. Typical language which is used to justify a possibility of reverter is: "so long as," "during," or "until." On the other hand, "a power of termination (also commonly called a right of re-entry) is that future interest which a transferor retains when he transfers an estate in his own favor." When a right of re-entry is created, the grantor or his heirs are given an election to terminate the estate upon the happening of an event. Language creating a right of re-entry may follow from: "provided that," "but if," or "upon the express condition."

Wheeler v. Monroe, 86 N.M. 296, 298, 523 P.2d 540, 542 (1974) (quoting Thomas F. Bergin & Paul G. Haskell, *Preface to Estates in Land & Future Interest* 64, 66 (1966)); *see also* 3 *Thompson on Real Property* §§ 24.01 (discussing possibilities of reverter), 25.01–.03 (discussing rights of entry) (David A. Thomas ed., 1994) (*Thompson on Real Property*).

The provisions of the Najeeb Deed are ambiguous. On the one hand, the condition is introduced by the phrase "provided however that." Normally this language is interpreted as creating a condition subsequent with the grantor and his heirs retaining the associated power of termination. *See* Restatement of Property § 45 cmt. j (1936) (Restatement). However, the condition itself contains language which indicates that the Najeeb Deed is to be "null, void, and of no effect," and that the land is to "revert to the grantor" upon occurrence of the condition. This language suggests that the condition is to operate automatically.

(7) Comment m to Section 45 of the Restatement notes, however, that "[s]uch a conveyance more commonly manifests an intent to create an estate in fee simple subject to a condition subsequent." The commentators addressing the subject agree with the Restatement's position. *See* Lewis M. Simes & Allan F. Smith, *The Law of Future Interests* §§ 247–48 (2d ed. 1956) (Simes & Smith). Representative cases so holding include *Hardman v. Dahlonega–Lumpkin County Chamber of Commerce,* 238 Ga. 551, 233 S.E.2d 753, 755–56 (1977); *Independent Congregational Society v. Davenport,* 381 A.2d 1137, 1139 (Me.1978); *Ohm v. Clear Creek Drainage District,* 153 Neb. 428, 45 N.W.2d 117, 119–20 (1950) (mere expression that the land shall revert is not enough by itself to create a possibility of reverter as distinguished from a right of entry), *Fausell v. Guisewhite,* 16 A.D.2d 82, 225 N.Y.S.2d 616, 617, 621 (1962) (holding where land was conveyed "subject to the following conditions and reservations viz: ... and whenever the property hereby conveyed shall cease to be used for school and meeting purposes ... the same shall revert to and become the property of the first part [sic]," a right of reentry was created); *but see Purvis v. McElveen,* 234 S.C. 94, 106 S.E.2d 913, 914–15 (1959) (concluding with little explanation that similar language created possibility of reverter).

We need not decide for our purposes here whether the Najeeb Deed conveyed a fee simple determinable or a fee simple on condition subsequent (though the latter is more likely). It is enough to recognize that it conveyed one or the other, thus reserving to the grantors and their heirs a property estate, either a possibility of reverter or a power of termination rather than an interest such as an easement or restrictive covenant...

Turning to the trial court's decision in this case, after considering the evidence the court denied Prieskorn's request for a decree quieting title to the property. It concluded that the circumstances surrounding Prieskorn's property had not changed to such a degree that it would be inequitable to enforce the reversionary clause, or that the purpose of the reversionary clause had been defeated. The court also concluded that, even if circumstances had changed, the changes were not so material as to render the purposes of the reversionary clause valueless to the area, or to make the benefits sought by the reversionary clause unobtainable. Finally, the trial court concluded "[t]hat the reversionary clause is a restraint on the use that may be made of the land subject to it and does not constitute a restraint on alienation." . . .

The Reversionary Provision Is Not an Unreasonable Restraint on the Alienation of the Subject Property

Prieskorn points to the fact that she was unable to sell her property at the price she would have liked to support her argument that the reversionary clause is an unreasonable restraint on alienation. She also claims she has been unable to purchase title insurance on the property because the reversionary clause creates an open question as to whether, in the event of a breach of the reversionary condition, all of the property would revert to the original owners if any part of the property is shown to violate the clause.

Prieskorn relies primarily upon our Supreme Court's decision in *Gartley v. Ricketts,* 107 N.M. 451, 760 P.2d 143 (1988), asserting that, under the factors set forth there, the reversionary clause in the Najeeb Deed is an unreasonable restraint upon alienation. The issue in *Gartley* was whether provisions in a deed ordering that the property in question be offered to a certain named person, or to that person's heirs or assigns, for a specified price before being offered for sale to others, was an unreasonable restraint on alienation. *See id.* at 452–53, 760 P.2d at 144–45.

The Court held that the provisions were unreasonable, primarily because they were of potentially unlimited duration and because "the number of persons to whom transfer [wa]s prohibited [wa]s very large," two of the several factors the Court looked to in making its determination. *Id.* at 454, 760 P.2d at 146.

In this case, in contrast, although the reversionary clause may be of unlimited duration, it does not direct to whom the property can or cannot be sold. Rather, it merely places restraints on the uses to which the owner can subject the property. "A restraint on the use that may be made of transferred property by the transferee is not a restraint on alienation. . . ." Restatement (Second) of Property: Donative Transfers § 3.4 (1983) (Restatement (Second)); *see also* 10 Richard R. Powell, *Powell on Real Property,* ¶ 842 n. 14, at 77–21 (1999) (*Powell on Real Property*). Some of the examples that accompany Section 3.4 of the Restatement (Second) aptly illustrate the difference between potentially invalid restraints on alienation and enforceable restraints on the use of property; they make clear that restraints on use, even though they may serve to limit the number of potential subsequent buyers, do not thereby become restraints on alienation. *See* Restatement (Second), *supra,* § 3.4 illus. 1–2.

To be sure, a restriction may restrain use in form but restrain alienation in substance, in which case it would be subjected to the reasonableness test articulated in *Gartley,* which is derived from the Restatement (Second). *See* 107 N.M. at 453–54, 760 P.2d at 145–46; *see also* Restatement (Second), *supra,* § 3.4 cmt. b & illus. 4. The difference may be difficult to discern. Indeed,

> [n]o precise rule can be formulated that will distinguish between restraints directed primarily at or having the primary effect of controlling the use of property, and restraints directed primarily at preventing the alienation of property. The form of the restraint is significant but not necessarily conclusive. The reasons for imposing the restraint, if discernible, may be relevant. The practical effect of the restraint may also be relevant. The restraint may have the effect of making the property more alienable than it otherwise would be.

Restatement (Second), *supra,* § 3.4 cmt. b; *accord Village of Los Ranchos de Albuquerque v. Shiveley,* 110 N.M. 15, 20–21, 791 P.2d 466, 471–72 (Ct.App.1989).

To the extent that Prieskorn presented any evidence at trial, however, to indicate that the primary purpose or ultimate effect of the reversionary clause was to restrain the alienation of the property, substantial evidence clearly supports the trial court's determination that the reversionary clause in the Najeeb Deed is a restraint upon the use of the property, and not a restraint upon the alienation of the property. There is no indication that the use restriction would make the property any less alienable than any other use restriction that might ultimately result in reversion of the property to the grantor upon breach of a condition subsequent.

Moreover, it appears that Prieskorn purchased the property with knowledge of the reversionary clause. Prieskorn's contention that she was unable to sell the property for the price she wanted does not require a decision in her favor. A lower sale price, in and of itself, does not make the restraint one of alienation rather than of use. *Cf. Shiveley,* 110 N.M. at 21, 791 P.2d at 472 (discussing municipality's power to restrict use of proposed subdivision's common area and stating: "[T]here is no indication that the restrictions on the common area would prevent buyers from purchasing the land or diminish the value of the property. In fact, the subdivision lots may be more valuable and desirable if the restrictions were enforced.").

Although Prieskorn is correct that *Gartley* sets forth factors for a court to use in determining whether a restraint upon alienation is reasonable, her reliance on *Gartley* is unavailing because the reversionary clause in the present case is not acting as a restraint on alienation. We therefore turn to Prieskorn's second issue—whether the trial court should have declared the reversionary clause invalid because the area around Prieskorn's property has changed to such a degree that enforcement of the clause would be inequitable.

The Trial Court's Decision is Supported by Substantial Evidence

Prieskorn argues that the use restriction in the Najeeb Deed is invalid because the circumstances in and around the subject property have changed to such a degree that enforcement of the reversionary provision would be inequitable. *See Whorton v. Mr. C's,* 101 N.M. 651, 653–54, 687 P.2d 86, 88–89 (1984). Defendants argue that the doctrine of changed conditions does not apply to the reversionary interest created in the Najeeb Deed because, under New Mexico law, the reversionary interest is a present, vested interest in them that cannot be taken away outside the terms of the conveyance.

Defendants may well have a point that the trial court erred in applying the doctrine of changed conditions in this case at all. The commentators and cases again appear to support the general idea that possibilities of reverter and powers of termination as estates in property are not subject to the doctrine of changed conditions. . . .

However, we do not reach that issue because substantial evidence clearly supports the trial court's findings and provides a ready basis for affirmance without requiring a definitive answer to the legal issue. The outcome is the same: the Najeeb Deed survives intact.

Among its findings of fact, the district court found the following:

11. That since 1950 the area around the Najeeb 71 acre tract has developed with a trailer park and a number of fairly expensive single family dwellings being built on a portion of the 71 acres; but more than half of the 71 acres is still vacant. A Walmart, a Hacienda Store, a Pizza Hut and several other commercial buildings, as well as a school and two churches, have been constructed within a block or two of the Najeeb land. The commercial buildings are primarily on the east side and partially on the south side of the Najeeb land, and the remainder of the land around the Najeeb land is residential.

13. That the reversionary clause has not prevented the building of several fairly expensive homes on the west side of the Najeeb land.

14. That since 1961, the Najeeb deed land has been subdivided into multiple ownership with a housing development of thirty (30) homes on the west end and a 204 unit mobile home park constructed by plaintiff's parents and predecessors on the east end. The center portion is undeveloped.

15. The changes in land use that have occurred in the 71–acre area subject to the reversionary clause and the surrounding area have not rendered the conditions of the reversionary clause without value to the area.

16. The changes in land use that have occurred in the 71–acre area subject to the reversionary clause and the surrounding area are not of such a nature as to have defeated the purposes of the reversionary clause's restrictions.

17. That plaintiff has been unable to sell her mobile home park for the price she wants, and she attributes this to the reversionary clause.

18. That there is no evidence that the sales prices of the other transactions involving the Najeeb deed land have been adversely affected by the reversionary clause.

From these findings the court concluded that any change in circumstances affecting the property since the conveyance were not sufficient to defeat or render the reversionary clause valueless to the subject property . . .

For the foregoing reasons, we affirm the decision of the trial court.

§ 4.8 THE RULE IN SHELLEY'S CASE

IN THE MATTER OF THE ESTATE OF HENDRICKSON

Superior Court of New Jersey, Chancery Div. Probate Pt. (1999).
324 N.J.Super. 538, 736 A.2d 540.

FISHER, P.J.CH.

It seems unimaginable that a court, near the end of this millennium, would be asked to consider the application of the long-abolished "Rule in Shelley's Case." Yet, this anachronistic doctrine—like Banquo's Ghost—has raised its hoary head and must be addressed not as an academic puzzle but as the key to a very real and substantial property dispute.

Wycoff Hendrickson ("Wycoff") died in 1928. His will, executed eight years earlier, states in part:

> I give and devise to my son Earle W. Hendrickson, my farm . . . during the term of his natural life . . . and *after the decease of my said son I give and devise the said farm to such person or persons as shall be his sole heir or heirs in land in fee simple*. . .

Earle Hendrickson ("Earle") died on May 31, 1997 setting in motion—after the passage of nearly 70 years—a dispute as to whether Wycoff, by this language, conveyed to Earle a fee simple (if the Rule in Shelley's Case applies) or merely a life estate (if it does not). If the former, defendants Elizabeth A. Olson and Nancy L. Nicholson ("Earle's devisees") are entitled to the property; if the latter, then the property passes to those who were Earle's heirs at the time of his death, namely, defendants Elizabeth S. Corson, Kathryn Deacon, Marie Field Sharbaugh, Carol Lynn Gasslein, Bonnie Joyce Weaver and Robert Weaver ("Earle's heirs").

Consideration of the Rule in Shelley's Case[5] seems odd because its place in the common law was abrogated in this State in 1934. But our

---

5. *Wolfe v. Shelley,* 1 *Coke* 93b, 76 *Eng. Rep.* 206 (K.B.1581). *Shelley,* however, is not the case which created "the Rule in Shelley's Case." As one of the leading commentators has said *Shelley* "rather takes the rule for granted, as well it might, for the rule has been recognized more than two hundred fifty years before as probably the

Legislature then declared only that the "rule of the common law, know as the Rule in Shelley's Case, shall not be applicable to any interest in property *created by any instrument to take effect hereafter.*" *N.J.S.A.* 46:3–14. Because Wycoff's will was probated in 1928, it remains unaffected by *N.J.S.A.* 46:3–14 ... Legislation prior to 1934 also deprived the Rule in Shelley's Case of some of its ancient vitality. In 1846, our Legislature declared its application barred when the life tenant died with surviving lineal descendants. Since Earle died without children, this legislatively-created exception to the Rule in Shelley's Case does not attach to the present circumstances. Thus the potential exists for the application of the Rule in Shelley's Case to Wycoff's will notwithstanding these legislative events ...

The Rule in Shelley's Case provides that "where an instrument GAVE A MAN A FREEHOLD and, by the same instrument, the remainder was given to his 'heirs,' the first taker had a fee simple if the remainder was to his heirs generally, and a fee tail if the remainder was to the heirs of his body." ... Here, the practical effect of the application or avoidance of the Rule in Shelley's Case can be summarized as follows: should the trust funds from the sale of the farm pass to the devisees in Earle's Will or to the persons who ended up being Earle's heirs? That is, did Wycoff's Will transfer to Earle a fee simple, which he could freely devise by way of his own Will, or did Wycoff merely devise a life estate which terminated upon Earle's death and would thereafter pass to certain persons, described as being Earle's heirs, by way of Wycoff's Will? Because Earle's devisees and his heirs are not the same persons, the application or avoidance of the Rule in Shelley's Case controls the disposition of the property.

The Rule in Shelley's Case is not only an anachronism—what one commentator referred to as " 'exhibit A' in the museum of legal antiques," I *American Law of Property* (1952), § 4.40 at p. 479—but a doctrine which runs contrary to all modern thought on the interpretation of wills.[6] It unabashedly causes a transfer of an interest in property greater than what may have been the actual or probable intent of the testator. *See, Page on Wills, supra,* § 37.15 at 618 (the intention of the conveyor is "ignored"); *American Law of Property, supra,* § 4.40 at p. 480 ("in nearly all instances of its application, it defeats the intent of the conveyor"); *Lippincott, supra,* 59 *N.J.L.* at 244, 28 *A.* 587 ("the intention of the testator ... is of no account whatsoever"); *Martling v. Martling,* 55 *N.J.Eq.* 771, 782, 39 *A.* 203 (E. & A.1896) (once found applicable, the

---

law, and it had become well established in English law some two hundred years before Shelley's Case was decided." 4 Bowe–Parker, *Page on Wills* (1961), § 37.15 at p. 618 (footnotes and citations omitted).

6. The purpose behind this 600 year old doctrine is elusive. While commentators have suggested a number of reasons for its creation, the rule is generally understood to have arisen in medieval England as a means to "prevent the use of a device which would otherwise deprive the overlord of the fruits of his seignory [seigniory]." *American Law of Property, supra,* § 4.40 at p. 478; *Page on Wills, supra,* § 37.15 at p. 619. In other words, it might have been analogous to any number of provisions which a modern day scrivener might insert into a document to avoid a taxable event.

Rule in Shelley's Case "cannot be controlled by any expression of a contrary intent"). Now, the overarching goal of current probate law is the application of the probable intent of the testator. *See, In re Englis' Estate,* 54 *N.J.* 350, 355, 255 *A.*2d 242 (1969) ("the modern view of will construction recognizes that the literal meaning of words will be departed from whenever necessary to carry out the intent of the testator as it appears from the entire document"); *Danelczyk v. Tynek,* 260 *N.J.Super.* 426, 428, 616 *A.*2d 1311 (App.Div.1992) ("the judicial function in construing a will is to ascertain and give effect to the probable intention of the testator"); *In re Klein's Estate,* 36 *N.J.Super.* 407, 408, 116 *A.*2d 53 (App.Div.1955) ("Will the court execute the clear intent of the testator which is not fully or definitely expressed in the will, or will it, by a strict technical adherence to the form of words and their literal meaning, or the absence thereof, suffer the discernible intention of the testator to be defeated?"). Examination of the Rule in Shelley's Case and its impact in 1999, thus, adds this further burden. It requires the court to inspect the parties' dispute not in the light of present day doctrine but in the shadows cast by the law existing in the 1920s.

As mentioned, in 1920, when Wycoff's Will was executed, and in 1928, when it was probated, the Rule in Shelley's Case was part of our common law. Considering its emergence from the mist of feudal England, it seems strange that the Rule in Shelley's Case would ever be followed in this country. But with our adoption of English common law, along came the Rule in Shelley's Case—a rule possessing no salutary purpose, surviving through the march of centuries only because of tradition and legislative inertia. Having no mission but to ensnare the unwary, it is hardly imaginable that a seasoned attorney in 1920 would have chosen words to intentionally invite application of the Rule in Shelley's Case.

A conveyance of a life estate with the remainder to the life tenant's heirs undoubtedly presupposes an intent to keep the property in the family after the death of the life tenant. It does not presuppose an intent to convey a fee simple; that could have been accomplished in this case, for example, by Wycoff simply saying "I give to Earle my farm" without the convoluted language quoted earlier. There can be no question, and the parties do not dispute, that Wycoff intended to give Earle only a life estate in the farm. But the Rule in Shelley's Case was designed to avoid the testator's intention to create both a life estate and a remainder interest in the life tenant's heirs by transforming the life tenant's interest into a fee simple. The challenge faced by the scrivener of a Will, during the reign of the Rule in Shelley's Case, was to capture the testator's desire to ensure the retention of the property in the family without tripping over the Rule in Shelley's Case. Scanning the landscape of New Jersey's common law at that time, Wycoff's attorney would have been confronted with a number of decisions of the State's highest court on the subject.

In 1896, the Court of Errors and Appeals found the Rule in Shelley's Case to attach to a devise to A for life, and "afterwards to descend unencumbered to his lawful heirs." As had been the understanding for centuries before, the Court described the rule as "one of law and not of construction," and disregarded the intention of the testator as being "of no account whatsoever." *Lippincott, supra,* 59 *N.J.L.* at 243–244, 28 *A.* 587 ... However, the last decision of the Court of Errors and Appeals on the subject—prior to the creation of Wycoff's Will—was *Peer v. Hennion, supra,* 77 *N.J.L.* 693, 76 *A.* 1084, where the Court found a particular choice of words to have successfully avoided application of the Rule in Shelley's Case.

An undiscerning eye might view as enigmatic the decisional law of this State at the time Wycoff's Will was drafted, executed and probated. But there is, contrary to the argument of Earle's devisees, a difference between the language which *Lippincott* and the others found to have caused the invocation of the Rule in Shelley's Case and the language which *Peer* found to have avoided it. For example, like the words examined in *Lippincott* mentioned above, the court in *Neill* considered a devise to A "and to go to his heirs at his death," 96 *N.J.Eq.* at 479, 126 *A.* 608, and in *Forman,* the conveyance was to A "for and during his natural life, and at his death to his heirs forever," 104 *N.J.Eq.* at 404, 145 *A.* 867. The language of the conveyances considered in *Martling, Armour* and *Woodbridge* is similar. A conveyance to "A for life and at his death to his heirs," so those courts said, compelled the application of the Rule in Shelley's Case notwithstanding the conveyor's contrary intent. But in *Peer,* the Court of Errors and Appeals found the doctrine did not attach to a slightly different provision, namely: to A "for and during her natural life, and after her decease I do give and devise to such person or persons as shall be her heir or heirs of land." 77 *N.J.L.* at 694–695, 76 *A.* 1084. In short, the difference between the decisions of the Court of Errors and Appeals in *Lippincott* and *Martling,* on the one hand, and *Peer,* on the other, can be summarized very simply. The conveyances in the former cases gave the remainder, after the life estate, to the life tenant's "heirs"; in *Peer,* the remainder was given to "such person or persons as shall be [the life tenant's] heir or heirs." That permitted the Court in *Peer* to conclude the testator was merely describing the persons to whom the remainder was conveyed and not persons to whom the property would descend. As the Court in *Peer* explained:

> If the testator in the present case had said "after her, Catherine's, death I do give and devise the said land to her heirs," it would have unmistakably created a fee in Catherine under the rule in Shelley's case; but the devise was not to her heirs. The devise of the remainder was to certain persons to be ascertained at the time of Catherine's death....
>
> Again, there seems to be significance in the fact that the testator, after declaring that Catherine's interest should endure during her natural life, should then employ the words: "I do give and devise the said land to such persons," & c. While, it is true, that if the devise had been to the heirs of Catherine, the employment of these words would not have been significant, yet, used as they are, as a separate

devise to certain designated persons, it would seem to indicate that the testator was creating a remainder by purchase.

We are of the opinion that the testator used the words "heir or heirs" as *designatio personarum* who should take the remainder; that those persons did not take by descent as heirs of Catherine, but by purchase from the testator; that the rule in Shelley's case does not apply, and that Catherine took an estate for life only.

77 *N.J.L.* at 696–697, 76 *A.* 1084. *Peer* had done it. *Peer*—or, rather, the attorney who drafted that Will—found the words which would talismanically ward off the Rule in Shelley's Case. Similarly, the Will drafted by Wycoff's attorney, and which Wycoff executed, gave the farm to Earle "during the term of his natural life," and after Earle's life, gave the farm "*to such person or persons* as shall be his sole heir or heirs in land in fee simple" (emphasis added). Wycoff invoked *Peer*'s words and avoided the Rule in Shelley's Case.

The argument of Earle's devisees that the Rule in Shelley's Case applies and that they are entitled to the property in question is rejected. Judgment will accordingly be entered.

§ 4.10 THE RULE AGAINST PERPETUITIES

Add as Note 9 on page 324:

In recent years there has been a trend to abolish the Rule in some states, such as Alaska and Idaho. See generally, Vallario, Death by a Thousand Cuts, The Rule Against Perpetuities, 25 J. Legis. 141 (1999). Dobris, The Death of the Rule Against Perpetuities, or the RAP Has no Friends—an Essay, 35 Real Prop. Prob. & TR.J. 601 (2000).

Chapter 7

LEASEHOLD ESTATES

§ 7.9 RETALIATORY EVICTION

Add to end of Note 7 on page 517:

Other factors in determining whether a retaliatory motive has dissipated, as noted in Hillview Associates v. Bloomquist, 440 N.W.2d 867, 871 (1989) are:

> In deciding whether a tenant has established a defense of retaliatory we consider the following factors, among others, tending to show the landlord's primary motivation was not retaliatory.
>
> (a) The landlord's decision was a reasonable exercise of business judgment;
>
> (b) The landlord in good faith desires to dispose of the entire leased property free of all tenants;
>
> (c) The landlord in good faith desires to make a different use of the leased property;
>
> (d) The landlord lacks the financial ability to repair the leased property and therefore, in good faith, wishes to have it free of any tenant;
>
> (e) The landlord was unaware of the tenant's activities which were protected by statute;
>
> (f) The landlord did not act at the first opportunity after he learned of the tenant's conduct;
>
> (g) The landlord's act was not discriminatory.

Restatement (Second) of Property §§ 14.8 comment f (1977).

§ 7.11 TERMINATION OF LEASEHOLD ESTATES AND REVERSION OF THE PREMISES

Add a new case immediately following Note 9 on page 556:

STONEHEDGE SQUARE LIMITED PARTNERSHIP v. MOVIE MERCHANTS, INC.

Supreme Court of Pennsylvania (1998).
552 Pa. 412, 715 A.2d 1082.

FLAHERTY, CHIEF JUSTICE.

The issue in this case is whether the landlord in a commercial lease is required to mitigate its damages when its tenant has breached the lease agreement by moving out before the end of the lease term.

Stonehedge Square Limited Partnership owns and operates a shopping center in Carlisle, Cumberland County, Pennsylvania. Stonehedge originally entered into a five year lease with General Video Corporation. The lease began on July 6, 1990 and ended on July 6, 1995. On July 31, 1992, General Video assigned its rights, duties and liabilities under the lease to Movie Merchants, Inc., which operated a video rental store on the premises from July of 1992 through October 27, 1994.

On or about August 25, 1994, Movie Merchants discussed with Stonehedge the possibility of terminating its lease prior to the expiration of the remaining term of the lease. Stonehedge listed the premises for rent, but was unable to find a tenant. Movie Merchants expressed a desire to buy out the lease, but no agreement could be reached as to a buyout amount. Stonehedge indicated to Movie Merchants that until a tenant could be secured, Movie Merchants was liable on the lease. On approximately October 27, 1994 Movie Merchants vacated the leasehold and failed to pay any rent thereafter.

Stonehedge then sued for rent due under an acceleration clause in the lease, seeking unpaid rent from November 1, 1994 to July 5, 1995. The case was tried without a jury, and on August 11, 1995, the court returned a verdict in favor of Stonehedge and against Movie Merchants in the amount of $46,797.09, plus interest. Movie Merchants excepted to the verdict and the trial court reversed itself, holding that the landlord had a duty to mitigate damages. Consequently, the court ordered a new trial on the issue of damages. Both parties appealed and the Superior Court reversed the order for a new trial and reinstated the original verdict in favor of Stonehedge. We granted the petition for allowance of appeal, limited to the issue of whether the Superior Court's reliance on our decision in *Auer v. Penn,* 99 Pa. 370 (1882), was proper. We now affirm.

Prior to the thirteenth century, leases were used for two purposes: to lend money and to facilitate the working of the land of prominent landowners. The first use of the lease, as a money lending device, originated as a way to avoid the ecclesiastical ban on usury. The borrower-landowner would receive money from the lender and would allow the lender to utilize his land for a certain period of time, presumably to grow crops. Subsequently, the money lending function fell into disuse and the agricultural lease, which was simply a device to provide a labor source for the production of crops, became prominent. In neither case was the tenant regarded as having an interest in the land. Both of these leases were important because they may have influenced the way in which early common law courts viewed tenants, viz., as having an action available on the contract, but no possessory action which would be dependent on the conveyance of an interest in the land. Thus, prior to the thirteenth century at common law, the tenant's interest in the land was personal and contractual, not a real property interest protected by a recovery of possession.

Between the thirteenth and sixteenth centuries, lessees gradually came to be regarded as holding an interest in the land and entitled to a possessory action. In fact, for purposes of giving the tenant a remedy to recover possession, the land interest came to be regarded as the only interest possessed by the lessee; the lease was regarded as essentially a conveyance rather than a contract.

In the last 150 years, the pendulum has begun to swing back so that contractual elements have once again assumed a role of importance in leases. A primary factor influencing this development is the urbanization of the population and the growth of cities, shifting the focus in leasing from land to the buildings on the land. Complexities in modern life and the increased importance of structures as opposed to the land itself commonly have been handled by provisions in leases. 2 *Powell on Real Property* § 16.02(1)(a).

Thus, in modern landlord-tenant law, leases have a dual nature, both as conveyances of protected property interests and also as contracts. Because of this historical background in which leases are sometimes viewed as conveyances and sometimes as contracts, problems in leases may be resolved either by principles of property law or by principles of contract law.

At common law, the mitigation of damages in a lease was regarded as being controlled by property law. Because the lease was a conveyance of real property, the tenant owned a non-freehold estate, and the landlord had no duty to mitigate damages arising from the tenant's breach of the lease. It was of no concern to the landlord whether the tenant chose to occupy the property or not. Cribbet, *Principles of the Law of Property,* p. 190 (Mineola, 1975). This was so in spite of the fact that it is a general principle of contract law that the non-breaching party to a contract has the duty to reduce his damages, if he can reasonably do so. Restatement of Contracts 2d, § 350. Nonetheless, Pennsylvania has followed the common law view that a non-breaching landlord has no duty to mitigate damages where the tenant has abandoned the property in breach of the lease.

In 1882 this court held that "if the relation of landlord and tenant was not ended by contract, he was not bound to rent to another during the term for relief of the defendant." *Milling v. Becker,* 96 Pa. 182 (1880). Two years later, in *Auer v. Penn,* this court held that "[t]he landlord may allow the property to stand idle, and hold the tenant for the entire rent; or he may lease it and hold him for the difference, if any." *Id.,* 99 Pa. 370, 375–76 (1882). And in 1928 this court held that "[r]eletting is not imposed on a landlord as a duty." *Ralph v. Deiley,* 293 Pa. 90, 141 A. 640, 643 (1928).

The issue becomes, then, whether we should now modify the rule of these cases. Movie Merchants argues that a lease is in the nature of a contract and is controlled by principles of contract law.[7] Further, it argues that the common law rule leads to unfair results, encourages waste, imposes penalties, and fosters bad public policy. Movie Merchants argues that although leases traditionally have been regarded as conveyances of land, modern leases are an exchange of promises, and contract law has long recognized the duty of a non-breaching party to mitigate damages.

Stonehedge, on the other hand, argues that the Pennsylvania rule should continue in effect because precedent requires it, because to require the landlord to mitigate damages would reward the breaching tenant for his breach, and because the requirement of mitigation would place an onerous burden on the nonbreaching landlord, denying him the benefit of his bargain.

We agree with Movie Merchants that certain aspects of leases are controlled by the law of contracts and that insofar as the law of contracts is applicable, the non-breaching party must mitigate his damages. In the *Pugh* case, supra, for example, the lease was construed as a contract; however, *Pugh* deals only with the issue of whether there is an implied warranty of habitability in a residential lease, and, therefore, offers us no guidance on the question of mitigation of damages.

For the following reasons, we now hold that a non-breaching landlord whose tenant has abandoned the property in violation of the lease has no duty to mitigate damages.

First, this rule is firmly established in Pennsylvania. As the *Auer* court stated:

> Nothing is better settled in Pennsylvania than that a tenant for years cannot relieve himself from his liability under his covenant to pay rent by vacating the demised premises during the term, and sending the key to his landlord.

---

7. In *Pugh v. Holmes,* 486 Pa. 272, 405 A.2d 897, 903 (1979), this court held that in a case involving the implied warranty of habitability, a lease is in the nature of a contract and is controlled by principles of contract law.

99 Pa. at 375. Leases have been drafted and bargained for in reliance on this rule. Business decisions and structured financial arrangements have been made with the expectation that this rule, which has been the law, will continue to be the law.

Second, the established rule has the virtue of simplicity. If the landlord is required to relet the premises, there is unlimited potential for litigation initiated by the tenant concerning the landlord's due diligence, whether the landlord made necessary repairs which would be required to rent the premises, whether the landlord was required to borrow money to make repairs, whether the landlord hired the right agents or a sufficient number of agents to rent the premises, whether the tenants who were refused should have been accepted, and countless other questions in which the breaching tenant is permitted to mount an assault on whatever the landlord did to mitigate damages, alleging that it was somehow deficient. This potential for complexity, expense, and delay is unwelcome and would adversely affect the existing schema utilized to finance commercial development.

Third, the Landlord and Tenant Act of 1951, Act of April 6, 1951, P.L. 69, art. I § 101 et seq., 68 P.S. § 250.101 et seq., which is a comprehensive regulatory scheme governing the landlord and tenant relationship, does not modify the landlord's duty to mitigate damages as it had been established in our cases.

Fourth, there is a fundamental unfairness in allowing the breaching tenant to require the nonbreaching landlord to mitigate the damages caused by the tenant. This unfairness takes the form of depriving the landlord of the benefit of his bargain, forcing the landlord to expend time, energy and money to respond to the tenant's breach, and putting the landlord at risk of further expense of lawsuits and counterclaims in a matter which he justifiably assumed was closed.

Fifth, in this case, the tenant was in a position to mitigate his own damages. The lease provides:

26. ASSIGNMENT AND SUBLETTING

The Tenant shall not, and shall not have the power to, transfer, assign, sublet, enter into license or concession agreements, change ownership, mortgage or hypothecate this Lease or the Tenant's interest in and to the Demised Premises without first procuring the written consent of the Landlord which Landlord may withhold in Landlord's sole discretion, not to be unreasonably withheld.

Thus, the tenant could have provided the landlord with a sublessee and the landlord had a duty not to unreasonably withhold consent. It seems self-evident that in choosing between requiring the non-breaching party and the breaching party to mitigate damages, the requirement, if any, should be placed on the breaching party, as it has been for centuries.

Order of the Superior Court is affirmed.

Add as a new case on page 558 before Notes and Questions:

AURORA BUSINESS PARK ASSOCIATES v. MICHAEL ALBERT, INC.

Supreme Court of Iowa (1996).
548 N.W.2d 153.

ANDREASEN, JUSTICE.

The district court entered judgment for the landlord on its action for the recovery of past unpaid rent and for future rent as damages under an acceleration clause in the parties' lease. The tenant contends that the acceleration clause constitutes an unenforceable penalty and that the court failed to award the proper damages. We affirm as modified and remand.

I. BACKGROUND FACTS AND PROCEEDINGS.

The defendants, Michael Albert, Inc. and Michael L. Albert (Albert), and the plaintiff, Aurora Business Park Associates, L.P. (Aurora), entered into a lease agreement in which Albert agreed to lease office and warehouse space in the Aurora Business Park. The lease term was from March 1, 1991 until February 28, 1996. Albert took possession of the property after signing the lease but vacated the premises some time in June or July of 1993. No June rent payment was made and notice of default was given to Albert. Shortly thereafter, Aurora served a notice to quit and retook possession of the premises. Aurora was unsuccessful in reletting the property.

The lease includes the following provision:

> In the event of termination of this Lease by reason of a violation of its terms by the Lessee, Lessor shall be entitled to prove claim for and obtain judgment against Lessee for the balance of the rent agreed to be paid for the term herein provided, plus all expenses of Lessor in regaining possession of the premises and the reletting thereof, including attorneys' fees and court costs, crediting against such claim, however, any amount obtained by reason of any such reletting.

In August 1993, Aurora brought an action to recover past unpaid rent and the balance of rent for the remaining term of the lease. The matter was tried before the district court on May 31, 1994. At the end of Aurora's case, Albert moved for a dismissal claiming Aurora failed to establish that it used reasonable diligence in attempting to relet the premises. The motion was denied. Albert also asserted that an award of future rent would be improper because the acceleration clause constituted an unenforceable penalty and, alternatively, that the court was required to offset any future rent by the reasonable value of the use of the premises to the landlord or a reasonable amount for rent the landlord would actually receive during the remaining term of the lease.

On August 31, the court entered judgment in favor of Aurora and against Albert in the amount of $221,692.28 with interest plus attorney fees and court costs. The court concluded that Albert had breached the lease by abandoning the property without giving notice and by defaulting on the rental payments. The court found the acceleration clause to be a valid liquidated damages provision rather than an unenforceable penalty. The court also found that Aurora had used reasonable diligence in attempting to relet the property. The court awarded damages for the remaining term of the lease without offset for a reasonable value of the use of the premises to Aurora or for rent which may be received from reletting the property during the remaining term of the lease. The court did not reduce the amount for future rent to its present value.

Albert filed a motion for a new trial. The court treated the motion as an Iowa Rule of Civil Procedure 179(b) motion and partially sustained Albert's motion by reducing the future accelerated rent payments to their present value. The court entered judgment for $215,251.90 with interest plus attorney fees and costs.

Our review is for correction of errors at law ... Whether a contract provision is a valid liquidated damages clause or an unenforceable penalty is a question of law for the court. *Rohlin Constr. Co. v. City of Hinton*, 476 N.W.2d 78, 79 (Iowa 1991).

II. Enforceability of the Acceleration Clause.

Albert contends that the judgment not only allows Aurora to recover the amount of rent due under the terms of the lease, but also allows Aurora to retain possession of the premises for its own use or relet the premises and retain any rents collected. Consequently, Aurora is placed in a better position than if the lease had been performed. Albert claims this not only violates the general principles of law against double recovery, but also violates the terms of the lease which specifically states that actual rents collected are to be offset against the amount of the claim. Additionally, Albert contends that the acceleration clause is an unenforceable penalty.

Some jurisdictions have held that provisions for the acceleration of payments of rent are invalid as unenforceable penalties. 49 Am.Jur.2d *Landlord & Tenant* §§ 716–17 (1995); *see, e.g., Kothe v. R.C. Taylor Trust*, 280 U.S. 224, 226, 50 S.Ct. 142, 143, 74 L.Ed. 382, 385 (1930) (lease provision that lessee's bankruptcy terminates lease and lessor is entitled to damages equal to rent for remainder of term is an unenforceable penalty); *Ricker v. Rombough*, 120 Cal.App.2d Supp. 912, 261 P.2d 328, 331 (1953) (rent acceleration provision in real property lease is unenforceable and void). Other jurisdictions, however, find specific acceleration clauses to be valid and enforceable. 49 Am.Jur.2d *Landlord & Tenant* §§ 716–17; *see, e.g., W & G Seaford Assocs. v. Eastern Shore Mkts.*, 714 F.Supp. 1336, 1346–49 (D.Del.1989) (acceleration clause for rent under commercial lease is valid liquidated damages provision); *Amacker v. Wedding*, 363 So.2d 223, 227–28 (La.Ct.App.1978) (landlord entitled to liquidated damages equal to rent for one year pursuant to commercial lease clause); *Frank Nero Auto Lease, Inc. v. Townsend*, 64

Ohio App.2d 65, 411 N.E.2d 507, 512 (1979) (weight of authority recognizes right of parties to contractually provide for repossession and acceleration of future rents where damages bear reasonable relationship to actual damages or lessor has obligation to mitigate damages); *Woodhaven Apartments v. Washington*, 907 P.2d 271, 273 (Utah Ct.App. 1995) (liquidated damages clause in residential lease is valid). The American Law Institute has recognized rent acceleration clauses as a valid expansion of a landlord's remedy:

> The parties may provide in the lease that if the tenant defaults in the payment of rent or fails in some other way to perform his obligations under the lease, the total amount of rent payable during the term of the lease shall immediately become due and payable.

Restatement (Second) of Property *Landlord & Tenant* § 12.1 cmt. k (1977).

Although Iowa has not addressed whether an acceleration clause for payments of rent constitutes a penalty, we have addressed related issues. *See Friedman v. Colonial Oil Co.*, 236 Iowa 140, 144–45, 18 N.W.2d 196, 198 (1945) (jury verdict for landlord who declared due, under an acceleration clause in commercial lease, the unpaid rent for the entire term of the lease was upheld on appeal although it appears the jury awarded damages only to the date of the trial). In *Hoefer v. Fortmann*, 219 Iowa 746, 259 N.W. 494 (1935), a farm lease which was for a term of three years with rent fixed upon a yearly basis contained the following provision:

> A failure to pay any portion of the rent as the same becomes due, or an abandonment of the premises or a breach of any of the covenants of this lease by second party, shall mature the whole amount of rent.

Hoefer, 219 Iowa at 748, 259 N.W. at 496. When the first year rent became due, the tenant did not pay. The landlord brought an action to recover the rent due at that time and judgment was entered against the tenant. The landlord then commenced a separate action to recover rent for the second year. The tenant argued that, because the acceleration clause made the entire rent for the three years become due upon the failure to pay the first year's rent, the landlord is barred from recovering the second year's rent. Because the lease was a yearly rental with the option of the landlord to terminate, we held that "the maturity of the rent for the year in which the breach occurred is the only rent as to which the maturity is accelerated thereby." *Id.* at 749, 259 N.W. at 496.

In *Becker v. Rute*, 228 Iowa 533, 535, 293 N.W. 18, 19 (1940), a commercial lease provided that any failure by the tenant "to comply with any of the terms and conditions of this lease shall make the whole amount immediately due and payable." The term of the lease was from May 1 to October 1 with rent payable as follows: $600 upon the execution of the lease, $1000 on May 1, and $500 on June 1, July 5, and 15. The tenant failed to pay the rent due on July 5 and 15. On July 20, the landlord brought an action for the past due rent. We affirmed the trial court which found the landlord, who declared a forfeiture for nonpayment of rent pursuant to a lease provision, was "entitled to judgment for rent that had matured prior to the forfeiture." *Becker,* 228 Iowa at 537, 293 N.W. at 20. Furthermore, we recognized that under the terms and conditions of the lease the landlord "had the right, which they did not exercise, to declare all the rent due." *Id.* at 538, 293 N.W. at 20.

A landlord and tenant may agree to the landlord's remedies if the tenant abandons the property and fails to pay rent, as long as the provision does not constitute a penalty. *See* Restatement (Second) of Property *Landlord & Tenant* § 12.1 cmt. j; *see also Benson v. Iowa Bake-Rite Co.,* 207 Iowa 410, 417, 221 N.W. 464, 467 (1928) ("The law seems quite settled . . . that parties to a lease may, by mutual consent, terminate the same, and if they do the tenant is not liable for future rent unless the same is stipulated for in the agreement terminating the lease."). We recognized the trend of favoring liquidated damages clauses in *Rohlin:*

> In the past, we disfavored the use of liquidated damage clauses and favored interpretation of contracts that make stipulated sums penalties. Later, we relaxed this penalty rule and recognized that parties may fix damages by contract when the amount of damages is uncertain and the amount fixed is fair.

Rohlin, 476 N.W.2d at 79. We adopted the following test:

> "Damages for breach by either party may be liquidated in the agreement but only at an amount that is reasonable in the light of the anticipated or actual loss caused by the breach and the difficulties of proof of loss. A term fixing unreasonably large liquidated damages is unenforceable on grounds of public policy as a penalty."

Id. at 80 (quoting Restatement (Second) of Contracts § 356(1) (1981)); *see also Engel v. Vernon,* 215 N.W.2d 506, 516 (Iowa 1974) ("if the sum stipulated is out of reasonable proportion to the loss or injury actually sustained or reasonably to be anticipated, it will be treated as a penalty"); *Golden Sun Feeds, Inc. v. Clark,* 258 Iowa 678, 682–83, 140 N.W.2d 158, 161 (1966); *McMurray v. Faust,* 224 Iowa 50, 58–59, 276 N.W. 95, 100 (1937).

We first address whether the amount of actual damages resulting from a breach of the lease were uncertain. If a breach occurs, the ability to obtain another suitable tenant for the property is unknown. If Aurora was able to relet the property shortly after the breach, the resulting damages would be reduced. There is no guarantee, however, that Aurora would be able to relet the premises at any time during the remainder of the lease term. Under this scenario, Aurora would suffer substantial damages. Furthermore, the damages will vary depending upon when the breach occurs. We find there is considerable uncertainty as to the actual amount of damages resulting from a breach of the lease two and one-half years before the end of its agreed term.

We next address whether the amount of liquidated damages under the acceleration clause is reasonable. The amount fixed in a liquidated damages provision "is reasonable to the extent that it approximates the loss anticipated at the time of the making of the contract, even though it may not approximate the actual loss." Restatement (Second) of Contracts § 356 cmt. b (1981); *see also Macal v. Stinson,* 468 N.W.2d 34, 36 (Iowa 1991) ("damages not reasonably anticipated by the parties when they contracted are not recoverable"). Albert contends that the proper measure of damages is the remaining rent due under the lease less the reasonable fair market value of the premises for the remainder of the term. Although other courts have utilized this formula, see 49 Am.Jur.2d *Landlord & Tenant* §§ 100, 103, we have not adopted this approach. In *Becker,* we rejected the tenants' argument that they "were entitled to credit on the rent due for the reasonable rental value of the use of the premises by [landlords] for the unexpired term." *Becker,* 228 Iowa at 539, 293 N.W. at 20–21.

A landlord is entitled to recover from a tenant the damages sustained as a result of the tenant's abandonment and nonpayment of rent. Restatement (Second) of Property *Landlord & Tenant* § 12.1 cmt. i; *see also* Iowa Code § 562A.32 (Under the Uniform Residential Landlord and Tenant Law "[i]f the rental agreement is terminated, the landlord may have a claim for possession and for rent and a separate claim for actual damages for breach of the rental agreement."). In general, the purpose behind the allowance of damages for breach of a contract "is to place the injured party in the position he or she would have occupied if the contract had been performed." *Macal,* 468 N.W.2d at 36. In Iowa "we are committed to the doctrine that when a tenant wrongfully abandons leased premises, the landlord is under a duty to show reasonable diligence has been used to relet the property at the best obtainable rent and thereby obviate or reduce the resulting damage." *Vawter v. McKissick,* 159 N.W.2d 538, 541 (Iowa 1968) ... *see also* Iowa Code §§ 562A.4(1) ("aggrieved party has a duty to mitigate damages"), 562A.29(3) ("If the tenant abandons the dwelling unit, the landlord shall make reasonable efforts to rent it at a fair rental."). Consequently, a landlord is entitled to damages equal to the amount of rent reserved in the lease, plus any other consequential damages, less amounts received in reletting the property. *See Roberts v. Watson,* 196 Iowa 816, 820, 195 N.W. 211, 212–13 (1923) (affirming judgment for landlord for full amount of unpaid rent plus subsequently accruing rent under five year lease less receipts from reletting); *CHR Equip. Fin., Inc. v. C & K Transp., Inc.,* 448 N.W.2d 693, 695 (Iowa App.1989) (allowing recovery of future rent payments, reduced to present value, under equipment lease which provided for reasonable damages); *see also Vibrant Video, Inc. v. Dixie Pointe Assocs.,* 567 So.2d 1003, 1004 (Fla.Dist.Ct.App.1990) (award of future rent for balance of commercial lease term less amount due from reletting must be reduced to present value).

The acceleration clause at issue here places Aurora in the position it would have occupied had Albert performed the entire lease. Furthermore, it takes into account the landlord's duty to mitigate damages by offsetting any claim by amounts received in reletting the property. We believe the acceleration clause reasonably approximates the anticipated or actual loss that resulted from Albert's abandonment and breach of the lease. Consequently, we hold that the acceleration clause is a valid and enforceable liquidated damages provision.

III. Credit for Rent Received by Reletting.

Albert urges the court should at least set off against the judgment any rents actually received by reletting the premises during the remainder of the lease. We agree. The acceleration clause explicitly provided a credit against the balance of the future rent for "any amount by reason of any such reletting." Furthermore, if a landlord regains possession of property abandoned by a tenant, courts "agree that a landlord may not keep both the accelerated rent and rent received from renting to a new tenant." Restatement (Second) of Property *Landlord & Tenant* § 12.1 n. 10; *see also W & G Seaford,* 714 F.Supp. at 1347 (Landlord "concedes that a lessor cannot recover possession of the premises and an amount representing solely accelerated rent."); *Quintero-Chadid Corp. v. Gersten,* 582 So.2d 685, 689 (Fla.Dist.Ct.App.1991) ("If the landlord goes back into possession and relets the premises, he must give the tenant credit for the rents received."); *see also* 22 Am.Jur.2d *Damages* § 712 (1988) (acceleration clause imposes a penalty "if it allows one party to repossess and resell, while still collecting the entire unpaid rental for the rest of the term").

IV. Disposition.

We affirm the district court's judgment upholding the acceleration clause in the parties' lease as a valid liquidated damages provision. We modify the court's decision to provide for a credit against the judgment for rents received from reletting the property during the remainder of the lease term. We remand the case for the district court to determine if the property was relet during the remainder of the lease term. If so, Aurora must credit Albert for the rents obtained. Costs of appeal are taxed one-fourth against Aurora and three-fourths against Albert ...

Chapter 8

"PRIVATE" CONTROLS OF LAND USE: SERVITUDES

§ 8.2 THE CREATION OF SERVITUDES

§ 8.2.4. Prescription

Append the following note on page 618:

9. In Boldt v. Roth, 618 N.W.2d 393 (Minn.2000) the neighbors who built a partially shared driveway were members of a single extended family—one land owner was mother-in-law to the other at the time the driveway was built. However, the mother-in-law subsequently transferred her property. The Minnesota Supreme Court held that the prescriptive period did not begin to run as long as the adjoining landowners were family members; but once the mother-in-law's property was transferred there was sufficient hostility to start the prescriptive period. The court reasoned:

> We have recognized that the general rule of presumed hostility is modified in cases in which family members own both the dominant and servient estates. See Wojahn v. Johnson, 297 N.W.2d 298, 306 (Minn. 1980). The reason for this modification is that the nature of close familial relationships is such that mere actual, open, exclusive, and continuous possession is not enough to give notice to a family member that a use is hostile.

The mother-in-law's conveyance of her land to a stranger had occurred more than fifteen years prior to the litigation. Apparently no survey was done and the buyer assumed that the entire driveway was on her property. In recognizing the creation of an easement by prescription the court explained:

> Once the owner of the servient estate is no longer a family member, actual and open use should suffice to notify the owner that the use is hostile. Subsequent servient estate owners who do not have a familial relationship have no reason to presume that a use is not an assertion of a claim of right. They have notice of the boundaries to their property and that the use is actual and open. We now ... hold that, absent evidence of continued permission, the transfer of the servient estate to a stranger renders hostile a use previously considered permissive due to a

close familial relationship and such transfer will commence the 15-year prescriptive easement time period....

Regardless of whether Boldt's original use of the driveway was permissive, that use became hostile in 1979 when Boldt's mother-in-law transferred the remaining parcel to nonfamily members.

Other decisions are far more likely than the *Fischer* decision in the casebook to find uses to be permissive. For example, in Coleman v. Keith, 6 P.3d 145 (Wyo.2000) the claimant owned landlocked property and used a road across adjoining land to reach it. He apparently never asked anyone's permission and spent money improving the roadway. In refusing to find prescription the Wyoming Supreme Court described its law this way:

> In Wyoming, the law requires a manifestation of hostile and adverse intent to use a road, even though it will likely result in revocation of permission to use the road across the neighbor's land. A person claiming a prescriptive easement may not rely on a presumption of adverse use or his subjective intent. Rather, the use is presumed to have been with permission. "To rebut this presumption the claimant must introduce evidence of the facts which demonstrate the manner in which the hostile and adverse nature of his use was brought home to the owner of the adjacent land." [quoting earlier decisions] Finally, the use must be inconsistent with the rights of the owner, such that the use would entitle the owner to a cause of action against the claimant, without permission asked or given.

The court then refused to find adverse use because the claimant was "never denied" permission to use the roadway. Further, "The predecessors in interest to the Keiths did not act to stop the Colemans from using the road, which supports a presumption of permissive use."

So how does one get a prescriptive easement in Wyoming? Apparently by showing that the land owner of the servient estate actually objected or actually denied permission to use the easement, and then neglected to bring a lawsuit for the prescriptive period even though the use continued.

§ 8.2.5. Recognition of Public Access Rights: Implied Dedication, Custom, and the "Public Trust"

Append this note on page 627:

5. In Leydon v. Town of Greenwich, 57 Conn.App. 712, 750 A.2d 1122 (Conn.App.2000) the town owned a public park that fronted on a beach. The town also had an ordinance that limited use of the park to residents, and the plaintiff was a non-resident. The court first held that those portions of the ordinance limiting park access to the town's residents were void on public policy grounds. It then found the Connecticut applied a public trust doctrine similar to that of New Jersey, that the park at issue was within the public trust, and as a result the town could not exclude the plaintiff from its park.

§ 8.4 TRANSFER OF OBLIGATIONS AND BENEFITS

§ 8.4.2. Real Covenants and Equitable Servitudes: Traditional Doctrine and Modern Deviations

Insert at the bottom of page 652:

With Wheeler v Schad, discussed in the second to the last paragraph on p. 652 of your casebook, compare the Virginia Supreme Court's decision in Sonoma Development, Inc. v. Miller, 258 Va. 163, 515 S.E.2d 577 (1999). The court found that the horizontal privity requirement had been met even though the real covenant sought to be enforced had been executed in a different piece of paper than the underlying deed. The two pieces of paper were executed on the same day, the declaration of restrictions was recorded, and the deed stated that it was made "subject to easements, restrictive covenants, restrictions and rights-of-way of record." The court said:

> With regard to the precise issue presented in this appeal, we conclude that horizontal privity did exist between the Schaers and the Millers. We are not willing to say that, in every situation, only one document can be examined in order to determine if horizontal privity existed between the original covenanting parties....
>
> In order to establish horizontal privity, the party seeking to enforce the real covenant must prove that "the original covenanting parties [made] their covenant in connection with the conveyance of an estate in land from one of the parties to the other." The Restatement of Property § 534(a) (1944), provides that horizontal privity is satisfied when "the transaction of which the promise is a part includes a transfer of an interest either in the land benefitted by or in the land burdened by the performance of the promise." In other words, the covenant must be part of a transaction that also includes the transfer of an interest in land that is either benefitted or burdened by the covenant.
>
> The term "transaction" is defined as "an act or agreement, or several acts or agreements having some connection with each other, in which more than one person is concerned, and by which the legal relations of such persons between themselves are altered." Black's Law Dictionary 1496 (6th ed.1990); cf. Virginia Housing Dev. Auth. v. Fox Run Ltd. Partnership, 255 Va. 356, 364–65, 497 S.E.2d 747, 752 (1998) (quoting Richmond Postal Credit Union v. Booker, 170 Va. 129, 134, 195 S.E. 663, 665 (1938)) (" '[N]otes and contemporaneous written agreements executed as part of the same transaction will be construed together as forming one contract.' "). In the context of the present case, we find that the transaction of which the covenant was a part commenced with the real estate contract between the Schaers and the Millers, and culminated with the deed conveying Lot 38 to the Millers. The "Declaration of Restriction" fulfilled the Schaers' contractual obligation to establish a restriction on Lot 39, which lot was being retained by the Schaers at that time, and was executed in conjunction with the deed to the Millers. Thus, it was part of a transaction that included the transfer of an interest in the land benefitted by the real covenant.

§ 8.4.3 Implied Burdens

Append this note on page 677:

3. In Hiner v. Hoffman, 90 Hawai'i 188, 977 P.2d 878 (1999) the Hawaii Supreme Court held that a covenant restricting a home in a subdivision to "one story" was unenforceable because it was too vague:

> Specifically, the ... Declarations, which contain the restrictive covenant at issue, fail to provide a definition or concrete dimensions for the term "story." The failure of the 1966 covenant to prescribe, in feet or by some other numerical measure, the maximum "height" of a "story" renders the language of the covenant ambiguous. As the Hoffmans point out, without such a definition, the "height restriction" of which the plaintiffs-appellees speak is meaningless. Thus, the Hoffmans argue that under the language of the 1966 covenant:
>
>> [a] two-story house, with each story being 25 feet tall, would be in compliance with the covenant, [whereas, a] three-story house, with each story being only 10 feet tall would violate the covenant[;] ... [y]et, the three-story house would have an overall height of only 30 feet while the two-story house would be 50 feet in height.

The court rejected the argument that local building codes, which defined a "story" as floor levels with a vertical distance between them of from six to twelve feet was adequate for purposes of the covenant.

A dissenter complained:

> The majority thus saves one story of a single house, but betrays years of reliance by the Hoffmans' neighbors and the larger Pacific Palisades community on the covenant's plain language and increases uncertainty and litigation with respect to other plainly worded covenants....
>
> The phrase "stories in height" is an ordinary, stock expression. The plain reading of "[n]o dwelling shall be erected ... which exceeds two stories in height," manifests the purpose of limiting structures to two stories or less—without regard or reference to exact "height" in feet and inches. It is undisputed that the Hoffmans' dwelling, built in a three-tiered, terrace-like form and described as "three-stories" by the Hoffmans themselves, is in fact three stories. One need not analyze any further or inquire into the height of the structure in feet and inches to determine that the Hoffmans' house strays from the common and conventional meaning of "two stories in height."

In Fong v. Hashimoto, 92 Hawai'i 568, 994 P.2d 500 (2000) the Hawaii court additionally held that a height restriction imposed on a downslope lot could not be enforced by the upslope lot owner unless the covenant in question expressly named the upslope lot as a beneficiary of the covenant. In this case only three of the lots in the fifteen lot subdivision had height restrictions, so the court was unwilling to find that there was a "general scheme" of height restrictions such that any lot owner in the subdivision could enforce the restriction against any other lot owner. Without the general scheme, that left enforcement to named beneficiaries and the court was unwilling to infer that an upslope lot was an intended beneficiary simply because it was the property whose view would be blocked in the event the burdened property owner built a structure in violation of the restriction.

Chapter 10

TAKINGS, DELIBERATE AND INADVERTENT

§ 10.1 EMINENT DOMAIN

§ 10.1.1 "Public Use"

Append to note 1, page 769:

In Manufactured Housing Communities of Washington v. State of Washington, 142 Wash.2d 347, 13 P.3d 183 (en banc, 2000), the Washington Supreme Court held that its own state constitution imposed a higher "public use" standard than the federal standard developed in *Hawaii Housing Authority*. It then held that a statutory right of first refusal given to mobile home park tenants to purchase their lot when it was put up for sale was an unconstitutional exercise of the eminent domain power for private rather than public use. Since this provision did not involve an explicit exercise of the eminent domain power at all, the court first concluded that it amounted to a regulatory taking, and then that the taking occurred for a private use. Both portions of that holding seem to go far beyond federal law.

The court emphasized that the right to sell property was one of the "bundle of sticks" contained in property ownership rights. While a compulsory right of first refusal did not force anyone to sell and did not affect the price of the transaction, it did deprive the land owner of the right to select its buyer. Although the seller wished to sell to X, the current tenant of the land in question could purchase instead by matching the price. But don't civil rights statute also interfere with a seller's right to pick her buyer? See Chapter 12 on housing discrimination law. Under those laws a seller cannot select a particular buyer on the basis of race, sex, or another protected classification. Of course, if the Washington Supreme Court should wish to declare that federal antidiscrimination law effected a taking its decision would be pre-empted under the Supremacy Clause.

§ 10.2 INVERSE CONDEMNATION

§ 10.2.2 *Taking by Regulation*

Insert the following Supreme Court decision and notes on page 839:

CITY OF MONTEREY v. DEL MONTE DUNES AT MONTEREY, LTD.

Supreme Court of the United States (1999).
526 U.S. 687, 119 S.Ct. 1624.

JUSTICE KENNEDY delivered the opinion of the Court.

This case began with attempts by the respondent, Del Monte Dunes, and its predecessor in interest to develop a parcel of land within the jurisdiction of the petitioner, the city of Monterey. The city, in a series of repeated rejections, denied proposals to develop the property, each time imposing more rigorous demands on the developers. * * *

The property which respondent and its predecessor in interest (landowners) sought to develop was a 37.6 acre ocean-front parcel located in the city of Monterey, at or near the city's boundary to the north, where Highway 1 enters. With the exception of the ocean and a state park located to the northeast, the parcel was virtually surrounded by a railroad right-of-way and properties devoted to industrial, commercial, and multifamily residential uses. The parcel itself was zoned for multifamily residential use under the city's general zoning ordinance.

The parcel had not been untouched by its urban and industrial proximities. A sewer line housed in 15–foot man-made dunes covered with jute matting and surrounded by snow fencing traversed the property. Trash, dumped in violation of the law, had accumulated on the premises. The parcel had been used for many years by an oil company as a terminal and tank farm where large quantities of oil were delivered, stored, and reshipped. When the company stopped using the site, it had removed its oil tanks but left behind tank pads, an industrial complex, pieces of pipe, broken concrete, and oil-soaked sand. The company had introduced nonnative ice plant to prevent erosion and to control soil conditions around the oil tanks. Ice plant secretes a substance that forces out other plants and is not compatible with the parcel's natural flora. By the time the landowners sought to develop the property, ice plant had spread to some 25 percent of the parcel, and, absent human intervention, would continue to advance, endangering and perhaps eliminating the parcel's remaining natural vegetation. * * *

In 1981 the landowners submitted an application to develop the property in conformance with the city's zoning and general plan requirements. Although the zoning requirements permitted the development of up to 29 housing units per acre, or more than 1,000 units for the entire parcel, the landowners' proposal was limited to 344 residential units. In 1982 the city's planning commission denied the application but stated that a proposal for 264 units would receive favorable consideration. In keeping with the suggestion, the landowners submitted a revised proposal for 264 units. In late 1983, however, the planning commission again denied the application. The commission once more requested a reduction in the scale of the development, this time saying a plan for 224 units would be received with favor. The landowners returned to the drawing board and prepared a proposal for 224 units, which, its previous statements notwithstanding, the planning commission denied in 1984. The landowners appealed to the city council, which overruled the planning commission's denial and referred the project back to the commission, with instructions to consider a proposal for 190 units.

[Further revision attempts, each conforming to new suggestions from the City, were met with further denials]

* * * After five years, five formal decisions, and 19 different site plans, respondent Del Monte Dunes decided the city would not permit development of the property under any circumstances. Del Monte Dunes commenced suit against the city in the United States District Court for the Northern District of California under 42 U.S.C. § 1983, alleging, inter alia, that denial of the final development proposal was a violation of the Due Process and Equal Protection provisions of the Fourteenth Amendment and an uncompensated, and so unconstitutional, regulatory taking.

* * *

[T]he District Court instructed the jury it should find for Del Monte Dunes if it found either that Del Monte Dunes had been denied all economically viable use of its property or that "the city's decision to reject the plaintiff's 190 unit development proposal did not substantially advance a legitimate public purpose." With respect to the first inquiry, the jury was instructed, in relevant part, as follows: "For the purpose of a taking claim, you will find that the plaintiff has been denied all economically viable use of its property, if, as the result of the city's regulatory decision there remains no permissible or beneficial use for that property. In proving whether the plaintiff has been denied all economically viable use of its property, it is not enough that the plaintiff show that after the challenged action by the city the property diminished in value or that it would suffer a serious economic loss as the result of the city's actions." With respect to the second inquiry, the jury received the following instruction: "Public bodies, such as the city, have the authority to take actions which substantially advance legitimate public interest[s] and legitimate public interest[s] can include protecting the environment, preserving open space agriculture, protecting the health and safety of its citizens, and regulating the quality of the community by looking at development. So one of your jobs as jurors is to decide if the city's decision here substantially advanced any such legitimate public purpose. "The regulatory actions of the city or any agency substantially advance a legitimate public purpose if the action bears a reasonable relationship to that objective." Now, if the preponderance of the evidence establishes that there was no reasonable relationship between the city's denial of the ... proposal and legitimate public purpose, you should find in favor of the plaintiff. * * *"

The jury delivered a general verdict for Del Monte Dunes on its takings claim, a separate verdict for Del Monte Dunes on its equal protection claim, and a damages award of $1.45 million.

* * *

The Court of Appeals affirmed. * * * In the course of holding a reasonable jury could have found the city's denial of the final proposal not substantially related to legitimate public interests, the Court of Appeals stated: "[e]ven if the City had a legitimate interest in denying Del Monte's development application, its action must be 'roughly proportional' to furthering that interest.... That is, the City's denial must be related 'both in nature and extent to the impact of the proposed development.' "95 F.3d, at 1430, quoting [Dolan v. City of Tigard, 512 U.S. 374, 391, 114 S.Ct. 2309, 129 L.Ed.2d 304 (1994)]

Although in a general sense concerns for proportionality animate the Takings Clause, see Armstrong v. United States, 364 U.S. 40, 49, 80 S.Ct. 1563, 4 L.Ed.2d 1554 (1960) ("The Fifth Amendment's guarantee ... was designed to bar the Government from forcing some people alone to bear public burdens which, in all fairness and justice, should be borne by the public as a whole"), we have not extended the rough-proportionality test of *Dolan* beyond the special context of exactions—land-use decisions conditioning approval of development on the dedication of property to public use. See *Dolan,* supra, at 385; Nollan v. California Coastal Comm'n, 483 U.S. 825, 841, 107 S.Ct. 3141, 97 L.Ed.2d 677 (1987). The rule applied in *Dolan* considers whether dedications demanded as conditions of development are proportional to the development's anticipated impacts. It was not designed to address, and is not readily applicable to, the much different questions arising where, as here, the landowner's challenge is based not on excessive exactions but on denial of development. We believe, accordingly, that the rough-proportionality test of *Dolan* is inapposite to a case such as this one.

The instructions given to the jury, however, did not mention proportionality, let alone require it to find for Del Monte Dunes unless the city's actions were roughly proportional to its asserted interests. The Court of Appeals' discussion of rough proportionality, we conclude, was unnecessary to its decision to sustain the jury's verdict. Although the court stated that "[s]ignificant evidence supports Del Monte's claim that the City's actions were disproportional to both the nature and extent of the impact of the proposed development," it did so only after holding that "Del Monte provided evidence sufficient to rebut each of these reasons [for denying the final proposal]. Taken together, Del Monte argued that the City's reasons for denying their application were invalid and that it unfairly intended to forestall any reasonable development of the Dunes. In light of the evidence proffered by Del Monte, the City has incorrectly argued that no rational juror could conclude that the City's denial of Del Monte's application lacked a sufficient nexus with its stated objectives." Given this holding, it was unnecessary for the Court of Appeals to discuss rough proportionality. That it did so is irrelevant to our disposition of the case.

The city challenges the Court of Appeals' holding that the jury could have found the city's denial of the final development plan not reasonably related to legitimate public interests. Although somewhat obscure, the city's argument is not cast as a challenge to the sufficiency of the evidence; rather, the city maintains that the Court of Appeals adopted a legal standard for regulatory takings liability that allows juries to second-guess public land-use policy.

As the city itself proposed the essence of the instructions given to the jury, it cannot now contend that the instructions did not provide an accurate statement of the law. In any event, although this Court has provided neither a definitive statement of the elements of a claim for a temporary regulatory taking nor a thorough explanation of the nature or applicability of the requirement that a regulation substantially advance legitimate public interests outside the context of required dedications or exactions, we note that the trial court's instructions are consistent with our previous general discussions of regulatory takings liability. See *Dolan*, supra, at 385; Lucas v. South Carolina Coastal Council, 505 U.S. 1003, 1016, 112 S.Ct. 2886, 120 L.Ed.2d 798 (1992); Yee v. Escondido, 503 U.S. 519, 534, 112 S.Ct. 1522, 118 L.Ed.2d 153 (1992); *Nollan*, supra, at 834; Keystone Bituminous Coal Assn. v. DeBenedictis, 480 U.S. 470, 485, 107 S.Ct. 1232, 94 L.Ed.2d 472 (1987); United States v. Riverside Bayview Homes, Inc., 474 U.S. 121, 126, 106 S.Ct. 455, 88 L.Ed.2d 419 (1985); Agins v. City of Tiburon, 447 U.S. 255, 260, 100 S.Ct. 2138, 65 L.Ed.2d 106 (1980). The city did not challenge below the applicability or continued viability of the general test for regulatory takings liability recited by these authorities and upon which the jury instructions appear to have been modeled. Given the posture of the case before us, we decline the suggestions of amici to revisit these precedents.

To the extent the city contends the judgment sustained by the Court of Appeals was based upon a jury determination of the reasonableness of its general zoning laws or land-use policies, its argument can be squared neither with the instructions given to the jury nor the theory on which the case was tried. The instructions did not ask the jury whether the city's zoning ordinances or policies were unreasonable but only whether "the City's decision to reject the plaintiff's 190 unit development proposal did not substantially advance a legitimate public purpose," that is, whether "there was no reasonable relationship between the city's denial of the ... proposal and legitimate public purpose." Furthermore, Del Monte Dunes' lawyers were explicit in conceding that "[t]his case is not about the right of a city, in this case the city of Monterey, to regulate land." * * * "They have the right to set height limits. They have the right to talk about where they want access. That's not what this case is about. We all accept that in today's society, cities and counties can tell a land owner what to do to some reasonable extent with their property".
* * *

Rather, the jury was instructed to consider whether the city's denial of the final proposal was reasonably related to a legitimate public purpose. Even with regard to this issue, however, the jury was not given free rein to second-guess the city's land-use policies. Rather, the jury was instructed, in unmistakable terms, that the various purposes asserted by the city were legitimate public interests.

The jury, furthermore, was not asked to evaluate the city's decision in isolation but rather in context, and, in particular, in light of the tortuous and protracted history of attempts to develop the property. Although Del Monte Dunes was allowed to introduce evidence challenging the asserted factual bases for the city's decision, it also highlighted the shifting nature of the city's demands and the inconsistency of its decision with the recommendation of its professional staff, as well as with its previous decisions. Del Monte Dunes also introduced evidence of the city's longstanding interest in acquiring the property for public use.

In short, the question submitted to the jury on this issue was confined to whether, in light of all the history and the context of the case, the city's particular decision to deny Del Monte Dunes' final development proposal was reasonably related to the city's proffered justifications. * * *

Thus, despite the protests of the city and its amici, it is clear that the Court of Appeals did not adopt a rule of takings law allowing wholesale interference by judge or jury with municipal land-use policies, laws, or routine regulatory decisions. To the extent the city argues that, as a matter of law, its land-use decisions are immune from judicial scrutiny under all circumstances, its position is contrary to settled regulatory takings principles. We reject this claim of error.

[On the right to a jury trial for damages the Court continued:]

Here Del Monte Dunes sought legal relief. It was entitled to proceed in federal court under [42 U.S.C.] § 1983 because, at the time of the city's actions, the State of California did not provide a compensatory remedy for temporary regulatory takings. See [First English Evangelical Lutheran Church of Glendale v. County of Los Angeles, 482 U.S. 304, 308–311, 107 S.Ct. 2378, 96 L.Ed.2d 250 (1987)]. The constitutional injury alleged, therefore, is not that property was taken but that it was taken without just compensation. Had the city paid for the property or had an adequate postdeprivation remedy been available, Del Monte Dunes would have suffered no constitutional injury from the taking alone. Because its statutory action did not accrue until it was denied just compensation, in a strict sense Del Monte Dunes sought not just compensation per se but rather damages for the unconstitutional denial of such compensation. Damages for a constitutional violation are a legal remedy [thus entitling the plaintiffs to a jury trial, rather than a purely equitable remedy where there is no such entitlement].

* * *

In an attempt to avoid the force of this conclusion, the city urges us to look not to the statutory basis of Del Monte Dunes' claim but rather to the underlying constitutional right asserted. At the very least, the city asks us to create an exception to the general Seventh Amendment rule governing § 1983 actions for claims alleging violations of the Takings Clause of the Fifth Amendment. See New Port Largo, Inc. v. Monroe County, 95 F.3d 1084 (11th Cir.1996) (finding, in tension with the Ninth Circuit's decision in this case, that there is no right to a jury trial on a takings claim brought under § 1983). Because the jury's role in estimating just compensation in condemnation proceedings was inconsistent and unclear at the time the Seventh Amendment was adopted, this Court has said "that there is no constitutional right to a jury in eminent domain proceedings." United States v. Reynolds, 397 U.S. 14, 18, 90 S.Ct. 803, 25 L.Ed.2d 12 (1970). * * *

Although condemnation proceedings spring from the same Fifth Amendment right to compensation which, as incorporated by the Fourteenth Amendment, is applicable here, * * * a condemnation action differs in important respects from a § 1983 action to redress an uncompensated taking. Most important, when the government initiates condemnation proceedings, it concedes the landowner's right to receive just compensation and seeks a mere determination of the amount of compensation due. Liability simply is not an issue. As a result, even if condemnation proceedings were an appropriate analogy, condemnation practice would provide little guidance on the specific question whether Del Monte Dunes was entitled to a jury determination of liability.

This difference renders the analogy to condemnation proceedings not only unhelpful but also inapposite. When the government takes property without initiating condemnation proceedings, it "shifts to the landowner the burden to discover the encroachment and to take affirmative action to recover just compensation." United States v. Clarke, 445 U.S. 253, 257, 100 S.Ct. 1127, 63 L.Ed.2d 373 (1980). * * * Where, as here, the government not only denies liability but fails to provide an adequate postdeprivation remedy (thus refusing to submit the question of liability to an impartial arbiter), the disadvantage to the owner becomes all the greater. At least in these circumstances, the analogy to ordinary condemnation procedures is simply untenable.

In actions at law predominantly factual issues are in most cases allocated to the jury. * * * Almost from the inception of our regulatory takings doctrine, we have held that whether a regulation of property goes so far that "there must be an exercise of eminent domain and compensation to sustain the act ... depends upon the particular facts." Pennsylvania Coal Co. v. Mahon, 260 U.S. 393, 413, 43 S.Ct. 158, 67 L.Ed. 322 (1922). * * * In accordance with these pronouncements, we hold that the issue whether a landowner has been deprived of all economically viable use of his property is a predominantly factual question. * * * [I]n actions at law otherwise within the purview of the Seventh Amendment, this question is for the jury.

The jury's role in determining whether a land-use decision substantially advances legitimate public interests within the meaning of our regulatory takings doctrine presents a more difficult question. Although our cases make clear that this inquiry involves an essential factual component, * * * it no doubt has a legal aspect as well, and is probably best understood as a mixed question of fact and law.

In this case, the narrow question submitted to the jury was whether, when viewed in light of the context and protracted history of the development application process, the city's decision to reject a particular development plan bore a reasonable relationship to its proffered justifications. As the Court of Appeals recognized, this question was "essentially fact-bound [in] nature." * * * Under these circumstances, we hold that it was proper to submit this narrow, factbound question to the jury.

We note the limitations of our Seventh Amendment holding. We do not address the jury's role in an ordinary inverse condemnation suit. The action here was brought under § 1983, a context in which the jury's role in vindicating constitutional rights has long been recognized by the federal courts.

[concurring and dissenting opinions by Justices Scalia and Souter are omitted]

Notes and Questions

1. Under *Monterey* a nontrespassory governmental act can be a taking even if it does not deprive the landowner of all economically viable uses of the land. A lesser injury can be a taking if its fails substantially to advance a legitimate public purpose. Is that a significant expansion of the takings rule developed in Lucas v. South Carolina Coastal Council, 505 U.S. 1003, 1016 (1992), reprinted in your casebook at p. 824? Suppose the property owner's injury is minor but the municipality's action is completely arbitrary and unjustified?

2. Note that the Court's statement on jury trials applies only to takings challenges brought under § 1983, which creates a separate damage action for constitutional violations by public officials acting under color of state law. In a § 1983 action a plaintiff must show that it has exhausted all available state remedies, and a state court today would have to operate under the rule of First English Evangelical Lutheran Church of Glendale v. County of Los Angeles, 482 U.S. 304, 308–311 (1987), compelling damages in an appropriate inverse condemnation case (see the Note on "Remedies for Unconstitutional Takings," casebook at 842). However, the *Monterey* case had been filed before the *First English* decision was handed down.

3. Recall the *Nolan/Dollan* analysis (see casebook at 791, 796) requiring a "quid pro quo" when the government insists on an easement or dedication of land in exchange for a right to develop. Does this requirement also apply when the quid pro quo that the government requests is an exaction of money or imposition of a regulatory burden rather than a dedication of land? See Benchmark Land Co. v. City of Battle Ground, 103 Wash.App. 721, 14 P.3d 172 (Wash.App.2000). The plaintiff received a

permit to enlarge and improve its business site on the condition that it expend substantial monies to improve its side of a city street adjoining the parcel. However, no land was to be taken from the plaintiff and no easement was to be dedicated to the public. The City relied on this language from the *City of Monterrey* case, supra:

> [The *Dolan* test] was not designed to address, and is not readily applicable to, the much different questions arising where, as here, the landowner's challenge is based not on excessive exactions but on denial of development. We believe, accordingly, that the rough-proportionality test of *Dolan* is inapposite to a case such as this one.

526 U.S. at 703.

Nevertheless, the Washington court rejected the city's argument "that *Nollan* and *Dolan* apply only when government, as a condition of approving the development, exacts a dedication of land," reasoning:

> The exaction here consisted of money, not land. The proper test to be applied here, according to the City, is that set out in *Penn Central Transportation Co. v. New York City*, 438 U.S. 104, 98 S.Ct. 2646, 57 L.Ed.2d 631 (1978), and *Agins v. City of Tiburon*, 447 U.S. 255, 100 S.Ct. 2138, 65 L.Ed.2d 106 (1980): whether the land-use regulation "substantially advances legitimate state interests and does not deny an owner economically viable use of his land." If the regulation meets these standards, it is not a taking.
>
> Both *Agins* and *Penn Central* dealt with restrictions on development and use of property. *Agins* was a challenge to a city zoning ordinance that required open space and limited the developer's five-acre parcel to five residences. *Agins*, 447 U.S. at 257, 100 S.Ct. 2138. The court held that, although the ordinances did limit the use of the property, they neither prevented the best use of the property nor extinguished a fundamental attribute of ownership. *Agins*, 447 U.S. at 262, 100 S.Ct. 2138. *Penn Central* involved New York City's ordinance establishing a program to preserve historic landmark buildings. *Penn Central*, 438 U.S. at 107, 98 S.Ct. 2646. The Landmarks Preservation Commission had denied Penn Central's proposals to construct an office tower atop Grand Central Terminal. *Penn Central*, 438 U.S. at 116–18, 98 S.Ct. 2646. Penn Central sued, claiming the City had taken its property without just compensation in violation of the Fifth Amendment. *Penn Central*, 438 U.S. at 119, 98 S.Ct. 2646. The court reiterated that the purpose of the Fifth Amendment is "to bar Government from forcing some people alone to bear public burdens which, in all fairness and justice, should be borne by the public as a whole." *Penn Central*, 438 U.S. at 123, 98 S.Ct. 2646 (quoting *Armstrong v. United States*, 364 U.S. 40, 49, 80 S.Ct. 1563, 4 L.Ed.2d 1554 (1960)). But the court noted in reviewing a number of zoning law decisions that it had "upheld land-use regulations that destroyed or adversely affected recognized real property interests." *Penn Central*, 438 U.S. at 125, 98 S.Ct. 2646. Concluding that the City's landmark preservation procedure substantially promoted the general welfare and afforded Penn Central reasonable use of its property, the court held that no taking had occurred. *Penn Central*, 438 U.S. at 138, 98 S.Ct. 2646.

In *Nollan,* the court faced a different problem. In that case, the government granted a permit to replace a small bungalow on a beach front lot on the condition that the owners provide an easement for beach travelers to cross the lot in traveling from one public beach to another. *Nollan,* 483 U.S. at 828, 107 S.Ct. 3141. The court held that the State's power to forbid the construction altogether (if necessary to achieve a legitimate state interest) must "include the power to condition construction upon some concession by the owner, even a concession of property rights, that serves the same end." *Nollan,* 483 U.S. at 836, 107 S.Ct. 3141. But the court held that the development condition (exacting the easement) violated the Takings Clause because it did not further the legitimate state interest (protecting the ocean view of passersby). Thus, there was no nexus between the condition and the problem the State sought to solve. *Nollan,* 483 U.S. at 838–39, 107 S.Ct. 3141. The court also noted that the State, to protect the public's view, could have restricted development of the property with a "height limitation, a width restriction, or a ban on fences." *Nollan,* 483 U.S. at 836, 107 S.Ct. 3141.

In *Dolan,* the government conditioned approval of a store expansion on dedication of land by the storeowner to provide a public greenway to combat flooding and provide a pedestrian and bicycle path. *Dolan,* 512 U.S. at 380, 114 S.Ct. 2309. The court found the necessary connection between the condition and the public problem, but it held that the government must also show that the condition required is roughly proportional to the development's impact on the problem that forms the State's legitimate interest. *Dolan,* 512 U.S. at 387, 391, 114 S.Ct. 2309. In reaching this conclusion, the court distinguished its earlier cases approving the government's authority to engage in land use planning. *See Dolan,* 512 U.S. at 385, 114 S.Ct. 2309. And one of these distinctions was that the conditions were "not simply a limitation on the use petitioner might make of her own parcel, but a requirement that she deed portions of the property to the city." *Dolan,* 512 U.S. at 385, 114 S.Ct. 2309.

Thus, *Nollan* and *Dolan* were unique in requiring dedications of real property. And they were also unique in another aspect. The government in neither *Nollan* nor *Dolan* restricted the use of the property to be developed. Rather, in each, the conditions required the developer to make an affirmative contribution to solve a public problem that existed, at least in part, outside the developed property.

Moreover, despite the language in *Del Monte Dunes,* the Supreme Court has applied a proportionality test when applying the Takings Clause in another setting. *See Eastern Enterprises v. Apfel,* 524 U.S. 498, 118 S.Ct. 2131, 141 L.Ed.2d 451 (1998). In *Eastern Enterprises,* the court considered a takings challenge to legislation requiring a former coal mine operator to fund health care benefits for retired miners and their beneficiaries. *Eastern Enterprises,* 524 U.S. at 514, 118 S.Ct. 2131. The legislative plan required former coal mine operators to fund benefits based on the operators' participation in earlier health care plans or employment of a qualified retiree in the past. Eastern was assessed premiums for a number of qualified retirees because of past employment. *Eastern Enterprises,* 524 U.S. at 517, 118 S.Ct. 2131. A plurality of the Court concluded that the legislative plan violated the Takings Clause because it "impose[d] severe retroactive liability on a limited class of parties that could not have anticipated the liability, and the extent of that liability is substantially disproportionate to the parties' experience." *Eastern Enterprises,* 524 U.S. at 528–29, 118 S.Ct. 2131. The plurality, in reviewing earlier decisions in the area, commented that "our decisions upholding the [Multiemployer Pension Plan Amendment Act of 1980] suggest that an employer's statutory liability for multiemployer plan benefits should reflect some 'proportion[ality] to its experience with the plan.'" *Eastern Enterprises,* 524 U.S. at 530, 118 S.Ct. 2131 (quoting *Concrete Pipe & Prods. of Cal., Inc. v. Constr. Laborers Pension Trust for S. Cal.,* 508 U.S. 602, 645, 113 S.Ct. 2264, 124 L.Ed.2d 539 (1993) (quoting *Connolly v. Pension Benefit Guar. Corp.,* 475 U.S. 211, 226, 106 S.Ct. 1018, 89 L.Ed.2d 166 (1986))). In short, the funding required of Eastern was a taking because the calculated amount was "unrelated to any commitment that the employers made or to any injury they caused...." *Eastern Enterprises,* 524 U.S. at 537, 118 S.Ct. 2131.

Although the condition exacted here was money, not land, we conclude that the *Dolan* proportionality test applies. The City, as in *Nollan* and *Dolan,* did not restrict the development of the property by limiting the number of residences, requiring wider streets in the property, requiring dedicated open space, imposing height limits or other similar conditions. Instead the City required the developer to address a problem that existed outside the development property—an adjoining street in need of improvement. And the development did not cause this problem, at most it only aggravated it.

Although *Del Monte Dunes* defines "exactions" as "decisions conditioning approval of development on the dedication of property," we emphasize the similarity of exacting land and money. If the government in *Nollan* and *Dolan* had exacted money rather than land and then purchased land to solve the problems, the same questions would arise: was the money exacted for and used to solve a problem connected to the proposed development? (*Nollan.*) And was the amount of money exacted roughly proportional to the development's impact on the problem? (*Dolan.*) Surely if the issues for an exaction of money are the same as for an exaction of land, the test must be the same: a showing of "nexus" and "proportionality."

We find no inconsistency between this analysis and the comment in *Del Monte Dunes* that *Dolan* was "inapposite." In *Del Monte Dunes,* the developer did not challenge the City's requirement that part of the land be set aside for a public beach, a buffer zone, a view corridor, and butterfly habitat. Rather, the developer claimed that the City did not intend to allow the development under any circumstances and sought to accomplish this goal through over-regulation. *Del Monte Dunes,* 526 U.S. at 699, 119 S.Ct. 1624. Thus, a *Dolan* proportionality analysis was inapposite in *Del Monte Dunes* because the government did not exact land or money.

Further, if the *Dolan* proportionality test does not apply, the government can exact conditions such as the one here with few limits. The condition advances a legitimate state interest-improving the public roads. And the condition does not deny the developer all economically viable use of its land. But the condition also seeks to force "some people alone to bear public burdens which, in all fairness and justice, should be borne by the public as a whole." *Armstrong,* 364 U.S. at 49, 80 S.Ct. 1563. It is this attempted transfer of a public burden that calls for a *Dolan* proportionality test.

Cf. Home Builders Assn. of Dayton v. City of Beavercreek, 89 Ohio St.3d 121, 729 N.E.2d 349 (2000), holding that the *Nollan/Dolan* test applied to a city's insistence on a cash payment, or "impact fee," in exchange for a right to develop, but in this case the requirement was satisfied.

§ 10.2.3 *Remedies for Unconstitutional Takings*

Append the following on page 845:

In Tahoe–Sierra Preservation Council v. Tahoe Regional Planning Agency, 228 F.3d 998 (9th Cir.2000), the Ninth Circuit refused to rehear its panel's earlier determination that a temporary moratorium on development did not give rise to a damages action under *First English Evangelical*. The panel reasoned that no taking had been proven to occur at all because the moratorium was only temporary. In dissenting vehemently from the refusal to grant a rehearing, Judge Kozinski and four colleagues protested that the panel effectively "overruled" *First English* by finding, not that damages are not due when a temporary taking occurs; but rather that no taking occurs at all when the government decision precluding development is only temporary. As Judge Kozinski noted, the government order banning development for three years denied the owner all economically beneficial use of his property during that period, and thus seemed to be encompassed within the Supreme Court's *Lucas* decision. At this writing the United States Supreme Court is considering a petition for certiorari.

Chapter 11

"PUBLIC" CONTROLS OF LAND USE: AN INTRODUCTION TO ZONING AND LAND USE PLANNING

§ 11.2 LEGITIMATE RATIONALES OF ZONING LAW

§ 11.2.1 *Federal Law: Zoning Limiting Expression, or Regulating Indecency and Excess?*

Add the following Supreme Court decision or substitute for the Buzzetti decision on page 865

CITY OF ERIE v. PAP'S A.M. DBA "KANDYLAND"

Supreme Court of the United States.
529 U.S. 277 (2000).

JUSTICE O'CONNOR announced the judgment of the Court....

On September 28, 1994, the city council for the city of Erie, Pennsylvania, enacted Ordinance 75–1994, a public indecency ordinance that makes it a summary offense to knowingly or intentionally appear in public in a "state of nudity."[8] Respondent Pap's, a Pennsylvania corpo-

---

8. Ordinance 75–1994, codified as Article 711 of the Codified Ordinances of the city of Erie, provides in relevant part:

"1. A person who knowingly or intentionally, in a public place:

"a. engages in sexual intercourse

"b. engages in deviate sexual intercourse as defined by the Pennsylvania Crimes Code

"c. appears in a state of nudity, or

"d. fondles the genitals of himself, herself or another person commits Public Indecency, a Summary Offense.

"2. "Nudity" means the showing of the human male or female genital [sic], pubic hair or buttocks with less than a fully opaque covering; the showing of the female breast with less than a fully opaque covering of any part of the nipple; the exposure of any device, costume, or covering which gives the appearance of or simulates the genitals, pubic hair, natal cleft, perineum anal region or pubic hair region; or the exposure of any device worn as a cover over the nipples and/or areola of the female breast, which device simulates and gives the realistic appearance of nipples and/or areola.

"3. "Public Place" includes all outdoor places owned by or open to the general public, and all buildings and enclosed

ration, operated an establishment in Erie known as "Kandyland" that featured totally nude erotic dancing performed by women. To comply with the ordinance, these dancers must wear, at a minimum, "pasties" and a "G-string." On October 14, 1994, two days after the ordinance went into effect, Pap's filed a complaint against the city of Erie, the mayor of the city, and members of the city council, seeking declaratory relief and a permanent injunction against the enforcement of the ordinance....

Being "in a state of nudity" is not an inherently expressive condition. As we explained in *Barnes*, however, nude dancing of the type at issue here is expressive conduct, although we think that it falls only within the outer ambit of the First Amendment's protection. See Barnes v. Glen Theatre, Inc., 501 U.S., at 565–566 (plurality opinion); Schad v. Mount Ephraim, 452 U.S. 61, 66, 101 S.Ct. 2176, 68 L.Ed.2d 671 (1981).

To determine what level of scrutiny applies to the ordinance at issue here, we must decide "whether the State's regulation is related to the suppression of expression." Texas v. Johnson, 491 U.S. 397, 403, 109 S.Ct. 2533, 105 L.Ed.2d 342 (1989); see also United States v. O'Brien, 391 U.S., at 377. If the governmental purpose in enacting the regulation is unrelated to the suppression of expression, then the regulation need only satisfy the "less stringent" standard from O'Brien for evaluating restrictions on symbolic speech.... If the government interest is related to the content of the expression, however, then the regulation falls outside the scope of the O'Brien test and must be justified under a more demanding standard.

The ordinance here ... is on its face a general prohibition on public nudity. By its terms, the ordinance regulates conduct alone. It does not target nudity that contains an erotic message; rather, it bans all public nudity, regardless of whether that nudity is accompanied by expressive activity. ...

Respondent and Justice Stevens[' dissent] contend nonetheless that the ordinance is related to the suppression of expression because language in the ordinance's preamble suggests that its actual purpose is to prohibit erotic dancing of the type performed at Kandyland. ...That is not how the Pennsylvania Supreme Court interpreted that language, however. In the preamble to the ordinance, the city council stated that it was adopting the regulation:

> " 'for the purpose of limiting a recent increase in nude live entertainment within the City, which activity adversely impacts and threatens to impact on the public health, safety and welfare by

places owned by or open to the general public, including such places of entertainment, taverns, restaurants, clubs, theaters, dance halls, banquet halls, party rooms or halls limited to specific members, restricted to adults or to patrons invited to attend, whether or not an admission charge is levied.

"4. The prohibition set forth in subsection 1(c) shall not apply to:

"a. Any child under ten (10) years of age; or

"b. Any individual exposing a breast in the process of breastfeeding an infant under two (2) years of age."

providing an atmosphere conducive to violence, sexual harassment, public intoxication, prostitution, the spread of sexually transmitted diseases and other deleterious effects.' "553 Pa., at 359, 719 A.2d, at 279.

The Pennsylvania Supreme Court construed this language to mean that one purpose of the ordinance was "to combat negative secondary effects."

As Justice Souter noted in *Barnes*, "on its face, the governmental interest in combating prostitution and other criminal activity is not at all inherently related to expression." 501 U.S., at 585 (opinion concurring in judgment). In that sense, this case is similar to *O'Brien*. O'Brien burned his draft registration card as a public statement of his antiwar views, and he was convicted under a statute making it a crime to knowingly mutilate or destroy such a card. This Court rejected his claim that the statute violated his First Amendment rights, reasoning that the law punished him for the "noncommunicative impact of his conduct, and for nothing else." In other words, the Government regulation prohibiting the destruction of draft cards was aimed at maintaining the integrity of the Selective Service System and not at suppressing the message of draft resistance that O'Brien sought to convey by burning his draft card. So too here, the ordinance prohibiting public nudity is aimed at combating crime and other negative secondary effects caused by the presence of adult entertainment establishments like Kandyland and not at suppressing the erotic message conveyed by this type of nude dancing. Put another way, the ordinance does not attempt to regulate the primary effects of the expression, i.e., the effect on the audience of watching nude erotic dancing, but rather the secondary effects, such as the impacts on public health, safety, and welfare, which we have previously recognized are "caused by the presence of even one such" establishment. Renton v. Playtime Theatres, Inc., 475 U.S. 41, 47–48, 50, 106 S.Ct. 925, 89 L.Ed.2d 29 (1986).

Although the Pennsylvania Supreme Court acknowledged that one goal of the ordinance was to combat the negative secondary effects associated with nude dancing establishments, the court concluded that the ordinance was nevertheless content based, relying on Justice White's position in dissent in *Barnes* for the proposition that a ban of this type necessarily has the purpose of suppressing the erotic message of the dance. Because the Pennsylvania court agreed with Justice White's approach, it concluded that the ordinance must have another, "unmentioned" purpose related to the suppression of expression. That is, the Pennsylvania court adopted the dissent's view in Barnes that "[s]ince the State permits the dancers to perform if they wear pasties and G-strings but forbids nude dancing, it is precisely because of the distinctive, expressive content of the nude dancing performances at issue in this case that the State seeks to apply the statutory prohibition." 553 Pa., at 359, 719 A.2d, at 279 (quoting *Barnes*, supra, at 592 (White, J., dissenting)). A majority of the Court rejected that view in *Barnes*, and we do so again here.

Respondent's argument that the ordinance is "aimed" at suppressing expression through a ban on nude dancing—an argument that respondent supports by pointing to statements by the city attorney that the public nudity ban was not intended to apply to "legitimate" theater productions—is really an argument that the city council also had an illicit motive in enacting the ordinance. As we have said before, however, this Court will not strike down an otherwise constitutional statute on the basis of an alleged illicit motive. *O'Brien*, 391 U.S., at 382–383; Renton v. Playtime Theatres, Inc., supra, at 47–48 (that the "predominate" purpose of the statute was to control secondary effects was "more than adequate to establish" that the city's interest was unrelated to the suppression of expression). In light of the Pennsylvania court's determination that one purpose of the ordinance is to combat harmful secondary effects, the ban on public nudity here is no different from the ban on burning draft registration cards in *O'Brien*, where the Government sought to prevent the means of the expression and not the expression of antiwar sentiment itself. . . .

Even if we had not already rejected the view that a ban on public nudity is necessarily related to the suppression of the erotic message of nude dancing, we would do so now because the premise of such a view is flawed. The State's interest in preventing harmful secondary effects is not related to the suppression of expression. In trying to control the secondary effects of nude dancing, the ordinance seeks to deter crime and the other deleterious effects caused by the presence of such an establishment in the neighborhood. See *Renton*, supra, at 50–51. In Clark v. Community for Creative Non–Violence, 468 U.S. 288, 104 S.Ct. 3065, 82 L.Ed.2d 221 (1984), we held that a National Park Service regulation prohibiting camping in certain parks did not violate the First Amendment when applied to prohibit demonstrators from sleeping in Lafayette Park and the Mall in Washington, D. C., in connection with a demonstration intended to call attention to the plight of the homeless. Assuming, arguendo, that sleeping can be expressive conduct, the Court concluded that the Government interest in conserving park property was unrelated to the demonstrators' message about homelessness. Id., at 299. So, while the demonstrators were allowed to erect "symbolic tent cities," they were not allowed to sleep overnight in those tents. Even though the regulation may have directly limited the expressive element involved in actually sleeping in the park, the regulation was nonetheless content neutral.

Similarly, even if Erie's public nudity ban has some minimal effect on the erotic message by muting that portion of the expression that occurs when the last stitch is dropped, the dancers at Kandyland and other such establishments are free to perform wearing pasties and G-strings. Any effect on the overall expression is de minimis. And as Justice Stevens eloquently stated for the plurality in Young v. American Mini Theatres, Inc., 427 U.S. 50, 70, 96 S.Ct. 2440, 49 L.Ed.2d 310 (1976), "even though we recognize that the First Amendment will not tolerate the total suppression of erotic materials that have some argu-

§ 11.2   INTRODUCTION TO ZONING LAND USE PLANNING   53

ably artistic value, it is manifest that society's interest in protecting this type of expression is of a wholly different, and lesser, magnitude than the interest in untrammeled political debate," and "few of us would march our sons or daughters off to war to preserve the citizen's right to see" specified anatomical areas exhibited at establishments like Kandyland. If States are to be able to regulate secondary effects, then *de minimis* intrusions on expression such as those at issue here cannot be sufficient to render the ordinance content based. . . .

This case is, in fact, similar to *O'Brien, Community for Creative Non—Violence,* and *Ward*. The justification for the government regulation in each case prevents harmful "secondary" effects that are unrelated to the suppression of expression. See, e.g., Ward v. Rock Against Racism, [491 U.S. 781 (1989)] at 791–792 (noting that "[t]he principal justification for the sound-amplification guideline is the city's desire to control noise levels at bandshell events, in order to retain the character of [the adjacent] Sheep Meadow and its more sedate activities," and citing *Renton* for the proposition that "[a] regulation that serves purposes unrelated to the content of expression is deemed neutral, even if it has an incidental effect on some speakers or messages but not others"). While the doctrinal theories behind "incidental burdens" and "secondary effects" are, of course, not identical, there is nothing objectionable about a city passing a general ordinance to ban public nudity (even though such a ban may place incidental burdens on some protected speech) and at the same time recognizing that one specific occurrence of public nudity—nude erotic dancing—is particularly problematic because it produces harmful secondary effects.

Justice Stevens claims that today we "[f]or the first time" extend *Renton*'s secondary effects doctrine to justify restrictions other than the location of a commercial enterprise. Post, at 1. Our reliance on *Renton* to justify other restrictions is not new, however. In *Ward*, the Court relied on *Renton* to evaluate restrictions on sound amplification at an outdoor bandshell, rejecting the dissent's contention that *Renton* was inapplicable. See Ward v. Rock Against Racism, supra, at 804, n. 1 (Marshall, J., dissenting) ("Today, for the first time, a majority of the Court applies *Renton* analysis to a category of speech far afield from that decision's original limited focus"). Moreover, Erie's ordinance does not effect a "total ban" on protected expression.

In *Renton*, the regulation explicitly treated "adult" movie theaters differently from other theaters, and defined "adult" theaters solely by reference to the content of their movies. We nonetheless treated the zoning regulation as content neutral because the ordinance was aimed at the secondary effects of adult theaters, a justification unrelated to the content of the adult movies themselves. Here, Erie's ordinance is on its face a content-neutral restriction on conduct. Even if the city thought that nude dancing at clubs like Kandyland constituted a particularly problematic instance of public nudity, the regulation is still properly evaluated as a content-neutral restriction because the interest in combating the secondary effects associated with those clubs is unrelated to the suppression of the erotic message conveyed by nude dancing.

We conclude that Erie's asserted interest in combating the negative secondary effects associated with adult entertainment establishments like Kandyland is unrelated to the suppression of the erotic message conveyed by nude dancing. The ordinance prohibiting public nudity is therefore valid if it satisfies the four-factor test from *O'Brien* for evaluating restrictions on symbolic speech. . . .

Applying that standard here, we conclude that Erie's ordinance is justified under *O'Brien*. The first factor of the *O'Brien* test is whether the government regulation is within the constitutional power of the government to enact. Here, Erie's efforts to protect public health and safety are clearly within the city's police powers. The second factor is whether the regulation furthers an important or substantial government interest. The asserted interests of regulating conduct through a public nudity ban and of combating the harmful secondary effects associated with nude dancing are undeniably important. And in terms of demonstrating that such secondary effects pose a threat, the city need not "conduct new studies or produce evidence independent of that already generated by other cities" to demonstrate the problem of secondary effects, "so long as whatever evidence the city relies upon is reasonably believed to be relevant to the problem that the city addresses." Renton v. Playtime Theatres, Inc., supra, at 51–52. Because the nude dancing at Kandyland is of the same character as the adult entertainment at issue in *Renton*, Young v. American Mini Theatres, Inc., 427 U.S. 50, 96 S.Ct. 2440, 49 L.Ed.2d 310 (1976), and California v. LaRue, 409 U.S. 109, 93 S.Ct. 390, 34 L.Ed.2d 342 (1972), it was reasonable for Erie to conclude that such nude dancing was likely to produce the same secondary effects. And Erie could reasonably rely on the evidentiary foundation set forth in *Renton* and *American Mini Theatres* to the effect that secondary effects are caused by the presence of even one adult entertainment establishment in a given neighborhood. See Renton v. Playtime Theatres, Inc., supra, at 51–52 (indicating that reliance on a judicial opinion that describes the evidentiary basis is sufficient). . . .

In any event, Erie also relied on its own findings. The preamble to the ordinance states that "the Council of the City of Erie has, at various times over more than a century, expressed its findings that certain lewd, immoral activities carried on in public places for profit are highly detrimental to the public health, safety and welfare, and lead to the debasement of both women and men, promote violence, public intoxication, prostitution and other serious criminal activity." The city council members, familiar with commercial downtown Erie, are the individuals who would likely have had first-hand knowledge of what took place at and around nude dancing establishments in Erie, and can make particularized, expert judgments about the resulting harmful secondary effects. . . .

Finally, it is worth repeating that Erie's ordinance is on its face a content neutral restriction that regulates conduct, not First Amendment expression. And the government should have sufficient leeway to justify such a law based on secondary effects. On this point, *O'Brien* is especially instructive. The Court there did not require evidence that the integrity of the Selective Service System would be jeopardized by the knowing destruction or mutilation of draft cards. It simply reviewed the Government's various administrative interests in issuing the cards, and then concluded that "Congress has a legitimate and substantial interest in preventing their wanton and unrestrained destruction and assuring their continuing availability by punishing people who knowingly and willfully destroy or mutilate them." There was no study documenting instances of draft card mutilation or the actual effect of such mutilation on the Government's asserted efficiency interests. But the Court permitted Congress to take official notice, as it were, that draft card destruction would jeopardize the system. The fact that this sort of leeway is appropriate in a case involving conduct says nothing whatsoever about its appropriateness in a case involving actual regulation of First Amendment expression. As we have said, so long as the regulation is unrelated to the suppression of expression, "[t]he government generally has a freer hand in restricting expressive conduct than it has in restricting the written or spoken word." Texas v. Johnson, 491 U.S., at 406....

The ordinance also satisfies *O'Brien*'s third factor, that the government interest is unrelated to the suppression of free expression.... The fourth and final *O'Brien* factor—that the restriction is no greater than is essential to the furtherance of the government interest—is satisfied as well. The ordinance regulates conduct, and any incidental impact on the expressive element of nude dancing is de minimis. The requirement that dancers wear pasties and G—strings is a minimal restriction in furtherance of the asserted government interests, and the restriction leaves ample capacity to convey the dancer's erotic message.... Justice Souter points out that zoning is an alternative means of addressing this problem. It is far from clear, however, that zoning imposes less of a burden on expression than the minimal requirement implemented here. In any event, since this is a content-neutral restriction, least restrictive means analysis is not required.

We hold, therefore, that Erie's ordinance is a content-neutral regulation that is valid under O'Brien. Accordingly, the judgment of the Pennsylvania Supreme Court is reversed, and the case is remanded for further proceedings not inconsistent with this opinion.

[Numerous concurring and dissenting opinions are omitted]

Notes and Questions

1. The *Erie* case effectively makes it possible for a city to exclude nude dancing everywhere within its boundaries. It need no longer justify its restrictions by showing that, while most of the city is closed to such activities, there are sufficient places remaining where it is lawful.

2. Is a statute that prohibits a certain type of activity everywhere, rather than simply designating limited places where it may occur, a "land use" provision? Cf. *Mount Laurel* (casebook 894), which involved a city ordinance that forbad apartment buildings or mobile homes anywhere in the City.

§ 11.2.2. The Role of State Law: Regulating Relationships and Aesthetics

Append the following note on page 888:

3. In Rolling Pines Limited Partnership v. City of Little Rock, 73 Ark.App. 97, 40 S.W.3d 828 (App.2001), the Arkansas Supreme Court upheld an ordinance that required a developer to show that a manufactured home (often similar to large mobile homes in design, but usually placed on permanent foundations) satisfy a standard that it be "compatible with and will not adversely affect other property in the area where it is proposed to be located." The ordinance then specified eight "minimum standards" for compatibility, namely, that such houses have:

> (1) a pitched roof of three (3) in twelve (12) or fourteen (14) degrees or greater; (2) removal of all transport elements; (3) permanent foundation; (4) exterior wall finished so as to be compatible with the neighborhood; (5) orientation compatible with placement of adjacent structures; (6) underpinning with permanent materials; (7) all homes shall be multi-sectional; and (8) off-street parking per single-family dwelling standard.

The plaintiff's housing proposal met the eight "minimum" standards but the defendant nevertheless concluded that this was insufficient to show compatibility under the circumstances. The court rejected the argument that a standard that measured compatibility by an unspecified standard in addition to the eight articulated requirements was void for vagueness, distinguishing *Anderson*:

> *Anderson* [v. City of Issaquah] involved an ordinance with phrases such as "harmonious," and "interesting," as well as "compatible," and the case was marked by numerous attempts on the part of the applicant to meet the board members' subjective concepts of acceptability. Because the board had to draw upon its own subjective "feelings" due to the absence of objective guidelines, the court held that the ordinance failed to pass constitutional muster.
>
> More on point is the decision in *Anderson v. Peden,* 569 P.2d 633 (Or.App.1977). As in the instant case, the municipal code designated mobile homes as a conditional use and included a "compatibility with the established neighborhood" standard. The court found that the phrase was not unconstitutionally vague. Also in *Life Concepts, Inc. v. Harden,* 562 So.2d 726 (Fla.Ct.App.1990), the court addressed a challenge to the term "compatible" and found that it was not impermissibly vague because it has a plain and ordinary meaning that could be readily understood by reference to a dictionary. We agree that the term has a well-defined meaning and is not so vague as to leave an applicant guessing as to its import or meaning. Moreover, there is no indication

that appellant was laboring under any misconception of what the ordinance required in order to obtain a permit. We conclude that appellant has not established that the ordinance is unconstitutional.

Are you convinced?

§ 11.4 SETTLED EXPECTATIONS AND THE ZONING PROCESS

§ 11.4.3. Nonconforming Uses

Append the following note on page 933:

5. In Balough v. Fairbanks North Star Borough, 995 P.2d 245 (Alaska 2000), the Alaska Supreme Court upheld an ordinance that granted nonconforming use status to junkyards, provided that the yards had been in compliance with all other building and use regulations prior to the zoning. In this case the plaintiffs' junkyard had not been properly fenced prior to the re-zoning and the effect was to deny it any nonconforming use status whatsoever.

Chapter 12

THE LAW OF HOUSING DISCRIMINATION

§ 12.3 HOUSING DISCRIMINATION AND FEDERAL LAW: THE 1866 CIVIL RIGHTS ACT AND THE 1968 FAIR HOUSING ACT

Append the following notes on page 980:

8. In Badami v. Flood, 214 F.3d 994 (8th Cir.2000), the Eighth Circuit held that the defendant violated the "familial status" provision of the FHA when he refused to rent to the plaintiff because of the plaintiff's large family (husband, wife and eight children), and that punitive damages were appropriate.

9. In Hack v. President and Fellows of Yale College, 237 F.3d 81 (2d Cir.2000), the court approved Yale's practice of forcing freshman to live in college dormitories, all of which were co-educational. The plaintiff's were orthodox jews, whose religious beliefs forbad them from living with members of the other sex. The complaint stated:

> By requiring the plaintiffs to pay for and live in rooms in co-educational residential colleges, despite the plaintiffs' religious objections to the sexual immodesty prevalent in Yale's dormitories, and by refusing to accommodate the plaintiffs' religious obligations, the defendants have discriminated against the plaintiffs, because of their religion, in the terms and conditions of a rental of a dwelling and in the provision of housing, in violation of the Fair Housing Act.

The court concluded that the plaintiffs were not being *denied* a housing opportunity because of their religion; rather, they were being forced to accept a housing opportunity that they did not want:

> The students do not allege that Yale's policy has resulted in or predictably will result in under-representation of Orthodox Jews in Yale housing. Therefore, their claim fails. We cannot read into their complaint the missing allegations crucial to a disparate impact claim

There was a long, historically thorough, and vigorous dissent.

§ 12.4 HOUSING DISCRIMINATION AND STATE LAW

Append to note 2 on page 987:

The courts are having an extraordinarily difficult time with the question of evangelical landlords who claim a religion-based right to exclude unmarried heterosexual couples from their housing. In McCready v. Hoffius, 459 Mich. 131, 586 N.W.2d 723 (1998), the Michigan Supreme Court reversed the lower court decision mentioned in your casebook (p. 987) and held that the landlord violated Michigan law by refusing to rent to unmarried couples. Further, the Michigan statute did not violate the landlords' right to the free exercise of their religious beliefs, under either the Federal or Michigan Constitutions. Subsequently, however, the court vacated that portion of its order holding that the Michigan statute did not violate the landlords' free exercise rights, and remanded to the lower court for further consideration of the question. McCready v. Hoffius, 459 Mich. 1235, 593 N.W.2d 545 (1999). And in Thomas v. Anchorage Equal Rights Comm., 165 F.3d 692 (9th Cir.1999), a Ninth Circuit panel held that a similar housing ordinance violated the landlords' rights of free exercise of their religion. However, the Ninth Circuit en banc then vacated that decision, holding that because the ordinance had not yet been enforced the question was not ripe for review. Thomas v. Anchorage Equal Rights Com'n, 220 F.3d 1134 (9th Cir.2000), cert. denied, 121 S.Ct. 1078 (2001).

†